5 VOCATIONAL PERSPECTIVES SERIES

alba house DIVISION OF THE SOCIETY OF ST. PAUL   STATEN ISLAND, N.Y. 10314

the challenge of "radical"

Renewal

Nicholas A. Predovich, S.J.

Preface by Bishop Joseph M. Breitenbeck, D.D.

Imprimi Potest:
Gualterus L. Farrell, S.J.
Provincial Superior of the Detroit Province

Nihil Obstat:
Austin B. Vaughan, S.T.D.
Censor Librorum

Imprimatur:
✝ Terence J. Cooke, D.D.
Archbishop of New York
July 5, 1968

The nihil obstate and imprimatur are official declarations that a book or pamphlet is free of doctrinal or moral error. No implication is contained therein that those who have granted the nihil obstat and imprimatur agree with the contents, opinions or statements expressed.

Library of Congress Catalog Card Number: 68-31514

Published, designed and produced in the U.S.A. by the Pauline Fathers and Brothers at Staten Island, N.Y., as a phase of their communications apostolate.

TO MARY
BRIDE AND VIRGIN
AND
TO ALL HER RELIGIOUS
DAUGHTERS AND SONS

PREFACE

The Holy Father, in an address given to the major superiors of Women Religious Institutes in Italy, encouraged them in their aims and recommended to them the needs of the Church: "We say nothing that you do not already know very well but we hope, by repeating it, to make it ever more convincing and worthy of continued reflection."

Father Predovich speaks for much the same reason. His *Challenge of "Radical" Renewal* is not an invitation to isolated experiments, but a description that bridges the subtle, continuing renewal that flows from the nature of the Church and today's revolutionary one that many have supposed to be from a new Spirit. His work is a continuing reflection set in an historical context that he uses originally and effectively.

In discussing vows, Father strikes upon the underlying conviction of his work — a vowed life springs from a glad love and gratitude. It is a glorification of God, a celebration of his goodness. Such a simple statement presupposes numerous preliminary agreements. The recent evolution of thought regarding the universal call to holiness is not omitted by the author, but recalled in a way that casts unifying light on the past, present, and future of religious renewal. With an understanding of the mentality and the background behind today's challenge, Father is neither threatened nor threatening.

He faces what is perhaps the single most important question challenging religious life today — why does it exist in the Church? Primarily, this way of life "foretells the resurrected state and the glory of the heavenly kingdom." This is its prophetic function — showing the future reality here and now and the inseparable love link between God and man. It is eternal love being lived out in faith and hope. "This much can certainly be said: the prophetic function of religious in the Church looks to a constantly growing, constantly evolving, constantly renovating reality. The prophetic thrust is to a future fulfillment."

The insight into the prophetic function is unique and the work states well its development and importance. The reader's challenge is how this future thrust is to be operative today.

Here St. Paul's grasp of each Christian's importance for the Church is applicable: "One may have the gift of preaching with wisdom given him by the Spirit; another may have the gift of preaching instruction given him by the same Spirit; and another the gift of faith given by the same Spirit." (1 Corinthians 12:8-9) A book such as *Challenge of "Radical" Renewal* is important for our Church for two reasons: its content is a comprehensive statement which shows ideas worthy of continued reflection; second, Father Predovich's concern and encouragement for religious is evident throughout. This makes response to this challenge both possible and promising.

The Most Rev. Joseph M. Breitenbeck, D.D.

Chairman of Bishops' Liaison Committee for Major Superiors of Women and Auxiliary Bishop of Detroit.

CONTENTS

INTRODUCTION

Why Write About the Challenge of Religious Renewal?

Changes galore have already affected religious life. Many of the changes have come not so much from a renewal in religious life itself as from what we can aptly call a new mankind and a new Church. For instance, mankind's concern with personalism, personality and personhood has certainly impressed itself on the laws, rules and customs of religious communities. Another insight of mankind, that a person cannot achieve self-fulfillment in isolation, has already shifted concern from the effects of common life to the meaning of community. The Church's concern for freedom of the person and for the dignity of every human being, already has an impact on the observance of obedience in religious life. That same concern for the dignity of the person is seen in the new liturgical stance in the present day theology, as it is also seen in the positive reference of Christians to the new morality — a primacy of charity morality.

How can one choose, from among all these wonderful and healthy changes, the most meaningful and the most essential? There is the rub! Some discretion has to be shown and definite selection made. The criterion I have used is very pragmatic; it does not follow from the relative importance of topics. For the most part choice of topic and method of development have been determined by the responses I have already had from religious. Every topic treated herein has been already proposed for thought, discussed, and criticized. Even though great interest has always been shown in the topic of renewal, the explanations and suggestions have not always been enthusiastically accepted. But this is the only way in which successful and meaningful changes can take place. Rather than stifling growth, dialogue and discussion and even disagreement are the fertile soil in which radical growth can take place.

When Pope John XXIII called for "going out" into the world, did he realize what this would mean to religious life in the Church? Probably not. But it was a charismatic out-pouring that triggered a response not only from the Church as a whole but specifically from the most charismatic People of God within the Church, namely, religious. No longer able to consider "the world" as something separate and apart; no longer willing to look upon "the world" as a foe or a source of temptation or a threat to sanctity; no longer able to fend against "the world" even behind cloister walls and aged ghettoes — religious have opened cloister cells and windows and doors and gates to . . ."the world?" Rather, to each other, really — to people; to fellow Christians; to mankind. The spirit behind these openings has begun to change the face of the earth. The atmosphere is fresh, healthy, invigorating. We're down to earth again. The "within" and the "without" are refreshed with the same gentle breezes. Religious have come alive.

In this "new birth" in a "new age" in which all men find themselves, surely everyone realizes the difficulties man encounters. Values, plans, goals, structures, laws, outlooks, even the very purpose of man's life — all are being re-evaluated. In the process of evaluation and change multitu-dinous difficulties have arisen. Yet, at the same time who of us can close our eyes to the opportunities that have also arisen as a result of the new development in the world, in the Church, and in religious life?

To change, to adapt, to renew, even to grow, calls for calculated risk. The element of risk has to be present in every instance of human growth. Man risks growth even with the food he eats. Even greater risk is demanded of the Christian as his faith evokes a greater calculated risk than any purely human act. So, too, with Christian love.

Love grows only when and if personal risk increases. For
the religious, already committed by vows to the greatest
risk of all — his whole being committed to Christ — calculated risk grows into a creative risk. Committed by vows
to a life of unmitigated responsibility, the religious should
not fear change nor be stymied by fear. Mature responsibility
for the religious demands creative risk. Creative risk has
made many religious anxious about change. But it should
be the same anxious concern and hopeful anxiety that the
coming of spring brings to us each year after the needed
inner-bound, snow-bound winter.

Religious, in this age, should realize that some changes
are inevitable — even drastic changes — and others come
about only by a creative and imaginative initiative. Nor are
changes always for the good, even after prolonged dialogue
and prudent decision. For the renewing religious no single
law or mode of operation or guideline will meet every
exigency. If, after changes have been made, we can still
say that within our religious community there is "as much
freedom as possible and as much restriction as is necessary,"
the very least we can say is that the soil for the growth of
truth, justice, and love has been prepared. Certainly, the
Spirit of God can best work in that kind of soil.

Today, no one doubts that we are living in an age of a
"new Pentecost." But I think that the doors of the cenacle
have been blown open by a revolutionary spirit. This was
needed because fear and insecurity were so very great.
Broken, helpless, and frightened by the blast and the noise,
religious have, like all Christians and all men, been forced
to look at their own existential world as a challenge, just
as the Apostles looked at their own world. Religious, I feel,
are beyond the stage in which there is a keen awareness of
disarray, of disorganization. Light is pouring in. Already,
they are singing a new hymn, a new song. It is to explain
the theme of this new hymn to love in religious life that the
following chapters are written.

one

Options and Structures

The spirit of the world today is change — change in outlook, change in form, change in method —change, change, change. No human institution has withstood this process of evolution. Even the Church of Christ, always subject to change and renewal has been subject to change at this moment of history even more than many other institutions. Yet, at the same time, the change in the Church is characterized by an element that is not always found in changing organizations. The change in the Church is radical, but not radical in the same sense as when we use the word to describe a person as "a radical." The radical change in the Church is marked by a re-examination, a re-looking at the original sources, the roots, from which it came. True, everything within the Church is questioned; the Church itself is questioned for that matter. Man, today, digs down to the very roots of being, down to the roots of the Church. And it is good, what he finds.

People of God:

As the Church looks once again at its origins, at the roots of its being and at its true meaning, one striking revelation seems to be most captivating: that the Church is the People of God. The Church, which is a mystery of Christ's revelation, cannot be adequately described or defined by any single metaphor.[1] But at the same time, one image or

---

1. Vatican II **Constitution on the Church,** #6. (Hereafter identified as Vat. II, **C.C.**)

figure may describe the Church at a certain period of history better than any other figure. The Church as the People of God best describes the Church in the world today. The Church, since its very foundation by Christ, has been bound solidly and firmly together into a unity. This unity, which is in Christ, with Christ, and through Christ, makes the Church a single people, the People of God. Every Christian united to that Church is no longer merely an individual, standing alone in the world. Nor is he any longer merely a person in vital contact with other persons. He is bound in, linked to, united with a single People of God. Every Christian, then, has chosen to be a member of this community, the People of God.

Vocation — Commitment:

How does he come to be part of this community, the People of God? He is called to it by God. The concept of a "call" from God can be expressed in different ways. Looking at the call from God's viewpoint, so to speak, we conceive of this call as a vocation, or as a grace of vocation, or as the will of God, or as God's grace being offered to each man and awaiting his response. On the other hand, man's response to this grace, this call from God, we designate as commitment. It is man's affirmation-response, man's "yes" response to God. In commitment, man is considered the active element. He responds to a call.

So, in a very real sense, vocation and commitment can be and often are two different aspects of one and the same reality. Whether we study the call of God to see how he takes the initiative or whether we study the response of man who commits himself by an answer to a call, we are often studying the same reality.

The call of God to each man comes at different times, in different ways, and in rather diverse circumstances. Seemingly, no two persons receive the call or answer it in exactly the same way. We can almost say that vocation and commitment are as unique as each of us is unique as a person. For this reason, the "kairos"— the opportune situation and condition in which vocation is realized and commitment made — may not always be pinpointed to a very specific moment of time. Man's "kairos" may take place in an existential moment, as it did when Saul converted to Paul, or in an extended existential encounter, as it did with Ignatius of Loyola during his Manresa experience.

Apart from any mere time element — in answer to the question of "when"— vocation and its counterpart, commitment, can be studied as a-temporal realities. They can be studied as realities apart from a relationship to any moment of time. They can be studied as realities that affect man's attitude, man's stance in the world in which he lives.

If we look at the vocation-commitment responses of man in this way, there are really three different levels of response. God's call to man is threefold: to be a man in this human condition; to live a life of Christian love; and to choose a particular state of life in which to live his life of love. Even though not every Christian can put his finger on the exact moment of time in which these calls come, every Christian, in one way or another, experiences them as realities.

Fundamental Option:

First of all, and the most fundamental of a person's vocations, is his call to be a man and to accept the human condition. God wishes every man to accept himself as man, to develop and fulfill himself as man. God freely gives each man his humanness, with all its aptitudes and qualities, and expects him to make himself fully human. God calls man, every man, just as he called the first Adam, to accept himself, direct himself, and perfect himself toward a fulfillment which God intended for him as man.

This call to be a "man," to accept the human condition, is not a call to an abstraction. Nor is it a call to accept a static nature or a "little self" within oneself. God calls each man to know and to accept the "self" that is more than just a soul and more than merely the Freudian ego. The "self" which man can accept or reject is the total individual person, the "who" that man is, in a present, here-and-now human condition.

It should not be too difficult to see that the fundamental option of man is not merely a momentary "yes" or "no" to God. The option is not merely an acceptance or a rejection of the human condition in a single moment of time. Such an option must be considered as the tone or the climate or the attitude of one's whole life. It is or becomes by one's free choice the basic perspective and the total concern of one's whole existence. One can almost say it becomes the deepest attitude and keenest sympathy of one's whole being.

The most important thing to realize is that this basic or fundamental option of man becomes an orientation of one's entire life. Such modern novelists as Updike and Bellow, and for that matter, a great number of contemporary novelists, have tried to describe this option in existential terms. In modern literature, perhaps, no one incarnates modern man's struggle in his commitment to the human condition better than Moses Herzog. But Herzog's specific response to the human condition is uniquely his own.

Man is free to accept or to reject this vocation. He is responsible for his own commitment to this vocation as man, this call from God. In fact, man's growth as a person depends on this basic, fundamental option he has of accepting himself as a person.[2] This self which man must accept or reject is his identity, his consciousness of being someone,

---

2. Cf. Pope Paul VI, **Development of Peoples**, #15, (Hereafter, identified as Paul, **Dev. Peop.**)

his experience of his own unique "being-in-the-world." No wonder that we must consider man's response to the option as an attitude or a tone of his life considered as an acceptance and as a development of the self.

Man's first and fundamental option demands that he have a basic knowledge of himself as a man, that he is conscious of himself as a unique self, and that he has a freedom to dispose of himself as a self. This consciousness of oneself as a self and of the freedom to dispose oneself are prerequisites for any of man's commitments. At the same time, since these prerequisites are so uniquely one's own, only the person himself can decide whether they are present. In the movie *Nobody Waved Goodbye,* for instance, Peter alone could decide the fundamental option of his own life.

Rejection or Acceptance:

On this level of fundamental option, man can reject himself and the human condition completely. By his own free decision, he can live the life of the grand delusion, the "as if" condition of one who refuses the responsibility of self-acceptance, growth, and self-disposition in the human condition. Man can freely close himself to further growth, to further fulfillment, and to any further call from God. He can say "no" to God. This danger of ego-centricity, of narcissistic self-centeredness, faces every man. Yielding to this danger can be the sin of any man. To stop here, to reject the growing "self," is to confine self-fulfillment to a very limited and self-centered ego.

In his response to the fundamental option man is equivalently saying he is not a static self-fulfiller. He says "yes" to more than this. When he accepts this basic option, he is affirming that he is created and called — expressed by an inner thrust — to a fulfillment that can complete itself only outside himself. By his affirmation from within, man is impelled by that dynamic, inner thrust to the without, to fulfill himself as a person. This can be done only in his experience of encounter with "the other."

On the level of fundamental option man makes a choice to accept and to be open to "the other," expressed as a single person or a group, just as he himself sees them to be. In this choice, man commits himself to "the other" just as "the other" is and lives and exists in the here-and-now human condition. Surely, this commitment can be a warm, noble, human response to one's fellow man. It is as if one commits himself to his fellow man in a here-and-now present reality. The horizon — if there is one — is very close, very near; the vision extends to an omega point that is realized in the future, surely, but merely on a horizontal level. This is the response to human love.

Love Option:

It is in man's opening of himself to this human condition, this opening of himself to "the other," that brings him face to face with a second option. Is the human condition self-contained with a place only for man and his development in the here-and-now or is there more? Can the "yes" saying of the fundamental option go beyond the present human condition? Is there some referent outside of what man sees of himself to which God has given man an option?

Man's second call, like the first, fundamental option, demands a response to "the other." But another reality comes into perspective. Something above and beyond catches the eye. Call it what you will — God revealing himself, Christ, Love, Spirit — it is a reality different from the merely human. In this free option, man, already disposed to "the other," realizes and accepts the reality of Something or Someone above and beyond the human condition or the human "other" to whom he commits himself.

The realization of such a reality may be expressed as something explicit or merely implicit. Its expression may be as vague as "God with us" or as vivid as "Christ present with us in our Eucharistic celebration." The man responding to this choice sees not only "the other"— his fellow man — but he also sees "an-Other." His omega point extends not only forward but also upward. Above and beyond the existential reality to which he commits himself, is a further reality. His commitment is both, through "the other" and with "the other;" his vision extends to a beautiful and uplifting horizon, not only a vision but a reality too . . . "an-Other."

The commitment to the first, fundamental option is a commitment to a here-and-now limited reality. The commitment very often is full, complete, sincere, open. But it is a commitment to only a partial reality. There is more to the existential human condition than a seeable, hearable, touchable here-and-now. The person who opens himself to "the other" in this way can freely close himself to a fuller growth on a higher level. He can refuse to respond to an offer to accept "an-Other" in a way that is not visible, audible, or tangible. This is a disposition of himself to which he is free and open, but he can choose to close himself to it.

Such a closing of the self and refusal for growth can lead into an aberration of love. Truly, one learns the art of loving, but at the same time there is always the danger that man begins to use others for his own love-growth, that others become objects to be used for growth. What should be "I-Thou" encounters that express and foster love turn into "I-It" encounters that attempt self-growth through "the other" and end in self-love.[3] Unless one's vision and one's hearing extend above and beyond what is merely seen and touched and heard, self-love is always a possibility.

---

3. This, to me, is the basic difficulty found in Erich Fromm's **The Art of Loving**. His "daring prescription for love" is not daring enough. His horizon of love is distant but not uplifting into a reality higher than the one standing before him to be loved. His is only a partial and dimmed vision of love.

A positive response to the love option, on the other hand, is an opening of oneself to a presence that in and through "the other" makes itself heard and felt and seen. For some this presence is an experienced encounter with Christ — the Christ of history truly, but now a risen Lord. For others, it is not as clearly heard or seen or felt. Nor can the presence of "an-Other" always be expressed in clear and distinct terms or words or even images. For the Christian — the man who responds positively to this new presence — there is always this problem: how to express this reality of a different Presence of "an-Other" without losing the aspect of its upward and beyond thrust? The Christian opens himself fully to love, but the object of the Christian's love is far above and beyond what eye has seen and ear has heard. This is the reason why it is so difficult to define or even describe.

But man is also free to give a negative response on this love option level. No author of our modern age has written more penetratingly than Albert Camus about the burdens and glories of our human condition. In his novel, *The Plague* for instance, the main action has to do with the responses of various people to this very love option. His other novels, too, in spite of the great variety of their characters, make it very clear that there are only two positive responses possible to any man: either he views life on the level of the fundamental option of the human condition or he commits himself also to something above and beyond.

Camus's decision, reflected in the characters he has created, is a "no" to this higher option. His characters, like Ivan Karamazov, allegorically represent any man who refuses to make the leap. They say "no" to the very things, the very option, to which the Christian says "yes."

The commitment of the Christian on this love option level can reach, if he so wishes, a very high degree of perfection. God has endowed every man and the human condition with many and wonderful qualities. By opening himself and by disposing himself to "the other," even on the fundamental option level, man can attain a high degree of perfection. The virtue of justice seems to be most operative on this level. Even love on this level seems to be conceived as a law, as something that is due "the other." But man has a call to more. In opening himself to union with the Risen Christ — the concrete and explicit expression of what is above and beyond — the Christian can attain a new fulfillment. By his option and the life he lives as a result, he can attain a fuller perfection, not at all possible to one of a lower level of commitment or to one who has refused the higher commitment.[4] Thus the Christian who is really and honestly living the love option in depth is by that very fact giving Christian witness. He will inevitably confront other men, and with a life that is itself a challenge, point to something that is above and beyond where they now take their stand.

State of Life Option:

Even though on this second level the Christian can attain the highest goal of his personal development, he still has an option open to him to choose a specific means to attain the highest goal. His third option consists of means to the desired end.

The third level of option, response, or commitment is open to the Christian alone. Only the man who is open to the above and the beyond of "an-Other" can either understand or dispose himself to this third option. It is the "state of life" option that has meaning and purpose and intelligibility only within the Christian context of being disposed to the above and beyond. To the Christian, only because he has disposed himself to the reality of "an-Other," there is left the option of how he wishes to dispose his openness and love to "the other." Either he can make the choice of "the other" as a married partner in a sacramental covenant of

---

4. Paul, **Dev. Peop.** #16.

marriage love or he can make the choice of "an-Other" in a covenant of virginal love.

Marriage, then, is but one of two choices on this third level. True, every person and not merely the Christian, is free to marry, to commit himself to a specific other. However, only the Christian can do this in a sacramental way, in a way that is a sign and a symbol for the Christian of the love of an "above and beyond" Other, namely Christ. For the non-Christian, marriage is a contract, and that is all. It is no sign or symbol pointing to a richer and fuller reality.

Man's second choice on this level can be to a life of virginity. Once again, for the non-Christian such a commitment has no meaning, for apart from its "above and beyond" orientation, virginity is sterile. But in its Christian context, virginity is not merely a sign and a symbol. Surely, it is a sign of the person's commitment to universal love. But commitment to virginity is more than just that. It makes here-and-now present a reality — a future state but now present in our midst. Virginity as a commitment makes the love of the "above and beyond" Other, a reality in the here-and-now human condition.

Former Structures Changed:

We can pause for a moment here and clarify a few difficulties caused by trying to force present shifting structures into past categories. Notice that what was formerly called a state of perfection and limited to what is here called the third option has been converted to the second level, the love option. Thus, perfection or holiness is an option open to every man and not merely to a few select Christians. Every person, and more so every Christian, is called to respond to love, and more particularly to the love of the risen Christ. Then too, what was formerly conceived of as three states of life is here conceived of quite differently. Every Christian, while still single and not commited to the specific means of either marriage or virginity, can attain holiness. On this second level of option, the Christian may well go through his whole life without specifying a particular state of life on the third option level.

It becomes evident, too, that in the past the expression "state of life" was used very ambiguously. For instance, we have often read of priestly state, lay state, religious state, and so forth. To clarify this confusion, the three levels of vocation, commitment bring out certain aspects of our Christian life that the expression "states in life" does not.

In a very meaningful way, Vatican Council II, extended the definition of religious life from a mere canonical construct to a fuller and richer biblical concept.[5] This evolution of structure makes it possible to conceive of the third option level as a choice between marriage and virginity, between a human family life or a religious community life. As we will see in a later chapter, virginity thus becomes the specific difference between the two choices on the third option level, the state of life option.

Priesthood and Celibacy:

What of the priesthood, then, as a state of life? Since Vatican II, we have to be much more cautious about how we use the term priesthood. We know now that every Christian, no matter how he is baptized in the Spirit, is "consecrated into a spiritual house and a holy priesthood." [6] Related to this common and holy priesthood, but nonetheless different in essence from it, is the ministerial or hierarchical priesthood. If we apply the phrase "state of life" to the ministerial priesthood, then we are not using the term "state" in the same way we use it when we refer to the three levels

---

5. Vatican II treated religious life quite extensively in two main decrees: **Constitution on the Church** and **Appropriate Renewal of Religious Life**.
6. Vat. II, C.C., #10.

of option open to the Christian. Why? The ministerial priesthood is just that — ministerial. It performs a function.[7] It is
a response on the part of a Christian to perform a specific
function among those who have responded to the Christian
vocation. The ministerial priesthood is an office, a function
of service in the Church, and can thus relate to both the
marriage option or the virginity option. Little wonder that
Vatican Council II had to clarify an issue by stating that
"the religious state of life is not an intermediate one between
the clerical and lay states."[8] The ministerial priesthood, as
an office with a function of service in the Church, can be
found in both the married life and the religious life.[9]

The question of priestly celibacy comes to mind immediately. This much can be said at this point. Some priests
respond to the canonical oath of celibacy in such a way
that they look upon it merely as an aid to performing their
function of service to the People of God in a fuller and more
meaningful way. Certainly, this is a beautiful response to
love of God and love of the People of God. But at the same
time, such a priest has not as yet committed himself to the
third option level of response. Other priests look upon the
canonical promise of celibacy in a much more meaningful
way. Their choice of celibacy is not merely another aid to
perform a function of service well. For them, celibacy takes
on the fuller dimension of religious commitment. Through
this deeper and fuller commitment they have made a
choice on the third option level. In terms of the shifting

---

7. The Church herself seems to be able to specify this function for at
least those who participate in the simple priesthood. Modern theologians,
for instance E. H. Schillebeeckx, O.P., maintain that "the derived participa-
tions in the apostolic office were not directly instituted by Christ. Christ
instituted directly the fullness of the priestly, i.e., episcopal, apostolic office."
(Laymen in the Church, p. 38, Alba House, 1963)

8. Vat. II, C.C., #43.

9. Consider, for instance, the long historical tradition of a married clergy
in Catholic rites other than the Western, Roman rite.

structures of the post-Vatican II Church they can be said
to be committed to a state of life option, the life of
virginity.[10]

Options and Ancient Analogies:

It may help somewhat to understand the three levels of
options by using some very ancient analogies as a structure.
The "field of God" and the "ancient olive tree" are two such
analogies. They can be used as symbols that give visual
structure to these realities (cf. figure number one).

First of all, man can make a free choice, which we have
called the fundamental option, as to whether he accepts
himself as a man in his present human situation and condition. He can make a free choice and dispose himself to be
in the "field of the Lord." Refusal of this option is man's
most fundamental sin. In the "field of the Lord" grows that
beautiful "ancient olive tree." The tap roots of this tree
are the prophets of old. The People of God make up the
stout and sturdy trunk of this olive tree. They have responded
positively to the love option. As a result all of them partake
of a common priesthood. Some, by free choice in response
to Christ's call, give special service through a hierarchical
priesthood. Then finally, the top of the olive tree divides

---

10. What has been stated here remains true even after the publication
of Pope Paul's **Priestly Celibacy.** A clear distinction has not always in the
past been drawn between policy and doctrine. In policy, the needs of the
People of God must always be uppermost. When Pope Paul decided that
priestly celibacy was still necessarily linked with the ministerial priesthood
in the Western Church, he was stating a matter of Church policy. A clearer
distinction between consecrated virginity as a personal choice in contrast
to priestly celibacy merely as an institutional policy will need more than
merely a change in Church practice. Rather, a deeper insight into a development of the revelation of Christ is needed. Otherwise, consecrated virginity
will not be considered a true state of life which demands a personal choice,
but rather a mere adjunct to one or other functional role in the Church.
The latter should not be stressed at the expense of the former.

into two mighty and graceful branches — both vitally full of the life and strength of the living trunk below. These two branches represent the state of life options. One branch

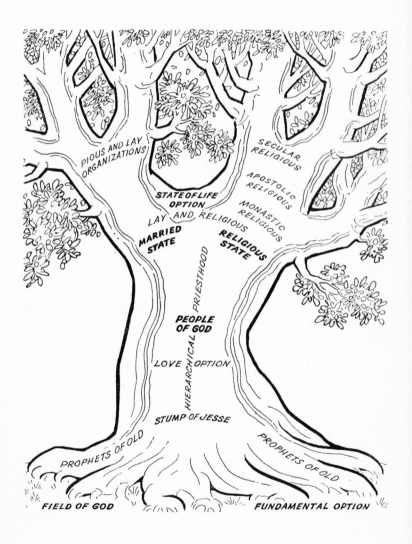

symbolizes those who have committed themselves to a sacramental marriage love. The second branch, equally strong and equally graceful, symbolizes those who have committed themselves, in one way or another, to the heavenly Father by their option to virginal love with Christ and for His Church.

The life of all thrives on the same energy, the same vitality, the same force from within. For all the People of God, this life, this energy, this vital force, this grace, this love — whatever we wish to call it — is the grace, the life, the love of Christ.

two

Religious Life in Salvation History

Canonical Structure or Inner Life?

Before Vatican II — and to some extent even after it — there was prolonged discussion and debate about the sources of religious life in the Church. Some writers, and among them some theologians, posed the question in this way: Was religious life merely a canonical structure, which the Church found useful in a period of Salvation History, or was religious life part of the inner structure of the Church because founded by Christ? Figuratively, was religious life a graft on the ancient olive tree or a tree branch? To argue in favor of the first part of the dilemma would mean the possibility of the demise of all religious life. If only a canonical structure, permitted in the Church because it served a useful purpose, then it was argued that perhaps the religious life has served its usefulness and should now give way to more useful and meaningful structures. Granting this supposition, religious life could be compared to the presence of cardinals in the Church. The time may come when they no longer serve a useful purpose and would give way to some other more useful structure. For instance, a Synod of Bishops might well, in time, perform all of the tasks that the cardinals do in the Church today. The question was posed then: could religious life, having served its purpose over the centuries, just fade away like the soldiers of the past?

Simply, beautifully, pointedly, the Fathers of Vatican Council II answered the dilemma. They cut the Gordian knot by posing the question in a much different way. For them, the problem was not a canonical structure but rather a question of how religious life fit into the whole life of holiness in the Church. The Fathers of Vatican II took religious life out of its canonical framework and, true to their own formula of renewal and adaptation, went back to basically biblical formulations. Freed from the limitations and confining structures of Canon Law, the Fathers of the Council saw religious life as a flowering out of holiness of the Church. They saw it as a very essential part of the Church, not as a sacramental part such as marriage, but a fuller expansion of the sacramental life of every Christian cleansed in the waters of baptism. Only in such a context could the Spirit inspire them to write thus about religious life: "Christ also proposed to his disciples that form of life which he, as the Son of God, accepted in entering this world to do the will of the Father."[1] To understand this insight of the Fathers of Vatican II in stating that religious life was the "form of life" proposed by Christ, some historical background is necessary. The meaning of vows, covenant, and commitment to Christ have to be seen in their historical context before they are seen as Vatican II saw them.

Historical Perspective of Vows:

Not too often, but often enough to be able to draw some conclusions, the Old Testament gives some striking examples of vow-taking. The vow of Jacob in the book of *Gen.* 28/16-22 and God's answer in *Gen.* 31/3 show how a man's vow was linked with man's need for God. So also the vow of Hannah in *I Sam.* 1/11 points to the same conclusion: a person in need turns to God in prayer and makes a covenant with God. There is always a loving and personal intimacy between man and God in such a vow. The expressed personal intimacy is an intense prayer in which the person who makes

---

1. Vat. II. **C.C.**, #44.

the covenant is very intimately united with the request. Prayer, a kind of real dialogue between the person and God, a form of commitment, a covenant-vow formula, faith in God that he will keep his promise — these are all elements linked with Old Testament vows.

There were evident developments in the Old Testament vow-making. For instance, what can be considered a vow-rite developed around the Nazirite — the "Nazir," who was segregated from the profane and dedicated to God.[2] Certain signs and symbols marked off the Nazirite — not drinking wine, not cutting his hair, etc.[3] Then too, a special kind of charism seemed to become associated with vows (*Am.* 2/11), and votive offerings became associated with vows (*Num.* 15/3; *Lev.* 22/18). Covenant and vow became responses of even a whole people, like Israel, rather than merely of individuals.[4]

Other elements can be seen, too. Men are free to take vows; no one can force such a commitment (*Dt.* 23/21-22). A person who takes a vow should not do so lightly (*Eccles.* 5/4-5). Vows are usually connected with the temple (*Dt.* 12/5-7). Such a response is always an act of gratitude (*Lev.* 6/1-21).

Perhaps nowhere in the Old Testament is the full significance of the ancient vow and covenant expressed in all its maturity as in the *Psalms*. Here, the "poor of Yahweh"— the "anawim"— the pious, devout, lowly seeker of the Lord expresses himself in praise, in gratitude, in glorifying God. As seen in *Ps.* 76/11, to make a vow means to glorify God. An "I need God" idea is expressed in *Ps.* 22, 56, and 116.

That God helps the man who vows himself comes out clearly in *Ps.* 66/13. But most important in the *Psalms* is

---

2. "Nazirite," **Dictionary of the Bible**, John McKenzie, S.J., p. 608.
3. Cf. Jg. 13/5.
4. See, for instance, the commitments of the Israelites of **Numbers, Leviticus,** and **Deuteronomy.**

the link expressed between the person making a vow and the community in whose presence the vow is made. For instance, the community presence is very evident in *Ps.* 116/14-18. Or again, *Ps.* 65 speaks of "in Sion," a biblical expression for the temple where the People of God meet. Most strikingly of all, in *Ps.* 22/22-26 almost all the Old Testament elements of vows are brought together — praise of Yahweh, the presence of the assembly or community, a liturgical setting, the person as part of the community, and the person witnessing to and for the community.

A few things seem to stand out in a study of the meaning of vows in the Old Testament. First, it is evident that some kind of development took place, not only with regard to the basic meaning of vows but also in regard to the relationship of the person and the community in which vows were taken. Secondly, the sign and symbol of the vows were not only personal but communal — vows became signs and symbols as much for the idividual as for the community. Thirdly, most of the features of the vows are found expressed in the *Psalms*.

New Testament Formula:

Surprisingly, neither the language, nor the liturgical expression, nor the formulas, nor the contexts of the Old Testament vows are found in the New Testament. How facile to conclude that vows and community responses to the vows of individuals were done away with by Christ and supplanted with a totally different kind of covenant — "a new covenant." The fact that Christ did not take upon himself or even propose to others the consecrated life of a Nazirite would, at first, seem to support such a conclusion. But, on the other hand, this was not the conclusion of Vatican II, which stated definitely in the *Constitution on the Church*: "Christ proposed to His disciples this form of life, which

He, as the Son of God, accepted in entering this world to do the will of the Father. This same state of life is accurately exemplified and perpetually made present in the Church."[5]

With the coming of Christ a new mystery was revealed and a new covenant or testament was made with the Father. Thus a new reality, the Church, came into existence. What was prefigured in the Old Testament was fully revealed in the New Testament. So too, the reality of one's consecration to God was changed. Vows took on a new signification. Just as "kahal" gave way to "ekklesia," so the life of the Nazirite gave way to the life of the evangelical counsels. Just as the Church was now a new reality in Christ, so the vows too, were a new reality in Christ.

How express the new concept? What words to use for this new reality? Perhaps one of the clearest New Testament texts is found in *Jn.* 17/19: "I consecrate myself for their sakes that they too may be consecrated."[6] St. John must have understood the full significance of this consecration, for he himself followed the example of Christ in this dedication. And yet, it is interesting to note that the Fathers of Vatican Council II did not refer to any specific biblical text when mention is made of Christ's proposal of a new consecration to his followers. The reason, most likely, is that all aspects of the life of Christ rather than merely a few words or texts have to be studied to understand the full significance of his consecration. Such a study yields the conclusion that in Christ's consecration are found all the elements of the Old Testament vows, and more. Total renunciation, praise of God, a personal prayer, reference to the community, a liturgical dimension, need and love for the Father — all are here. Yet, it is evident that Christ did not follow the consecrated life of a Nazirite or the penitential life of either

---

5. Vat. II., C.C., #44.

6. For a rather comprehensive study of the meaning of this consecration, see **In the Redeeming Christ**, F. X. Durrwell, C.Ss.R., Chapter I.

John the Baptist or the Essenes. His was another way, a more excellent way.

Christ did reveal a new way, a specifically different kind of consecration by vows to God. In his revelation we find two distinct modes of consecration — marriage and virginity. The latter is Christ's specific contribution to a New Testament revelation. Through a consecration to virginity, a new aspect of the mystery of God is revealed to man. This is what Christ himself chose, and this is the new way he proposed to his followers.

Christ's State of Life Option:

The love option to which Christ calls every Christian, as we have seen, is the commitment to love one another as he has loved us. With this basic commandment expressed, Christ proposes a further twofold state of life option — marriage or virginity. In marriage the Christian gives beautiful witness to an aspect of Christ's love; marriage is a sign, a witness to Christ's present love for his Church. Marriage in Christian love takes on a sacramental sign and value. In sacramental marriage the here-and-now love of Christ for his People, the Church, is signified. But no human reality or timely creature can exhaust, even in sign, the fullness of the mystery of God's love for us. To manifest to us another aspect of that tremendous mystery, Christ reveals to his Church a new reality, Christian virginity. Christian marriage and Christian virginity are revealed as aspects of this mystery most clearly in one pericope of the New Testament, *Mt.* 19/9-12. There is no question of superiority or contrast or relationship expressed here. Rather, two state of life options are proposed, both as specific responses to love. Both are good; both are ways of serving God. "Virgins chosen with respect to the kingdom of God" reveals an aspect of the mystery of God to his Church not revealed to us in a sacramental sign, such as marriage.

Pauline Concepts:

St. Paul also made a definite contribution to understanding this revelation. He himself, like St. John, responded personally to this invitation by Christ to virginity. Paul explains his consecration in the *First Letter to the Corinthians*, Chapter 7. He contrasts marriage and virginity, states that not all are called to the state of virginity, and shows that through the consecrated virgin the risen Lord, himself a virgin, is present in a special way. For Paul, the virgin gives witness to the reality of Christ's presence — a realized eschatology. A future "eternity-love" is now a present reality, witnessed to by virginal consecration. Paul enthusiastically affirms that Christ's love for the People of God is not merely something that is an actuality here on earth. This same love will continue for all eternity — such is our faith. But that faith in Christ's eternal love can now be expressed in a present fact, witnessed to by the expressed love of a consecrated virgin.

St. Paul saw clearly that both marriage and virginity manifested different aspects of God's love for his People. He saw, too, the beauty of the sacramental sign of marriage, so rich in its signification. At the same time, Paul was not blind to the effects of sin, especially original sin, among men. He saw clearly how easy it is for man to substitute a created, even a physical reality for the totality. Thus, even though marriage should be uplifting, sweeping man up to the divine, still there is a constant weight pulling man down, holding man down in his ascent to a personal union with God.[7] Man in marriage needs the uplifting witness of the consecrated virgin; the consecrated virgin needs the sign of marriage to see the love that Christ has for the existential human condition.

---

7. Cf. **A Heart to Know Thee**, E. J. Cuskelly, M.S.C., pp. 78-ff.

Historical Development:

For a full and complete understanding of the two state of life responses optioned by the Christian, an historical dimension should be added to this study. But such an historical treatment must be left to the competence of the Church historian. However, even at the present time and under very limited analysis, from this mass of historical developments, some conclusions can be drawn. For instance, in the entire history of the Church through twenty centuries, there is evidence of an interplay between two polarities — the witness of the Church to the "eternity-love" features of the mystery of God and, at the other pole, the witness to the "incarnational love" features of the mystery of God. The constant dynamic pull and attraction of these two polarities is, really, the history of the Church. From this same interplay of the two polarities, the "eternity-love" and the "incarnational-love," a powerful dynamism has pushed forward in history an evolving and ever-renewing life centered around the commitment to virginity. From the virgins who gathered around Christ, to the followers of St. Paul, to the hermits of the desert like Paul and Anthony, through the time of Pachomius and Basil, up to and beyond the solitude and silent enclosures of Benedict, to Dominic and Francis, to the active charism of an Ignatian community — a real growth process has been going on. In the various forms of religious life that developed over these centuries, there is a richness, a variety, a beauty, almost an infinite adaptability. Work and prayer, activity and contemplation, mobility and enclosure, in the world and apart from the world, alone and with community — there seems to be no end to the possible variations.[8]

---

8. Vat. II. **Appropriate Renewal of Religious Life,** #12 and 20. (Hereafter identified as Vat. II, **A.R.R.L.**).

And yet, there is a very evident development or pattern of development that has taken place. The development is an on-going process, continuing right at the present time. The patterns of development, obviously, were not too evident in the beginning. But now, with twenty centuries of history and with the theological perspective of development opened by Vatican II, these patterns stand out quite clearly.

A closer look at the history of religious life in the Church reveals that since the time that Christ founded this life, three rather basic forms of religious life have developed. Traditionally, these forms or modes of religious life have been called monastic life, apostolic religious, and more recently, secular institute. True, at the beginning, the structures of these three forms were not too clearly outlined. Even now, after a much clearer delineation by Vatican II, it may be a bit difficult to draw a fast and clear line between one or other type of religious life. Yet, on the whole, these are the three major forms of religious life in the Church. Who is to say, really, which of the forms came first in the Church? Historically, the monastic form received its structure in the Church before the other two forms. It took a Dominic, a Francis, and an Ignatius to give structure and shape to the form of apostolic religious life.[9] And not until *Provida Mater* of Pius XII in 1947 did the secular institute receive official form in the structure of the Church. On the other hand, who is to say that variations of these three basic forms have not been found at least seminally in the Church from the very beginning? Today, we can more easily and more clearly situate religious communities into this structure. Yesterday, religious life was being lived in various ways, but the structure was not as evident.

---

9. For a brief history of apostolic religious life see The Apostolic Life, Marie Hubert Vicaire, O.P. Fr. Vicaire's treatment does not take into account St. Ignatius' specific contribution to the development.

If we revert back to the symbol of the ancient olive tree, we recall that the tree branches off into two mighty arms at the top. These two branches represent the two state of life options. Now, we can see that the branch of religious life spreads out into a triple division. At the base of the branch is monastic life; blending into this and growing out further is the apostolic religious life. And finally — newest and greenest at the end of the branch — is the secular religious life.[10] All forms are filled with and flow with the life of the Church. All add something to the revelation of that eternal mystery, the Trinitarian God-life. All are symbols of one or other aspect of that profound mystery.

10. "Secular religious" will hereafter be used to designate a member of a secular institute. Thus, the three forms are monastic, apostolic, and secular religious.

three
Why Religious in the Church?

The question is quite legitimate: Why do we have to have religious — priests, brothers, and sisters — in the Church? To answer this question there is obviously a need for a clearer and a better understanding of the meaning of religious life not as presented to us as a canonical construct but rather in a more theological setting. As seen already, religious life is not merely a canonical addition to the life of the Church. However, the Church has raised the religious profession to a canonical state and has given religious institutes canonical status, fully recognized by the Church.[1] But the dignity of such a recognition by the Church does not change the essential relationship of religious life with the Church. It does not make religious life merely a canonical state.

Then too, it is very important to realize that the response of a Christian to the religious life does not put him on *the only* way to perfection. Religious life is a way, a means to holiness, but not *the only* means to holiness. This should be clear to all after reading the *Constitution on the Church.* This causes some confusion since in the past the response to the life of religious vows was identified with the "state of perfection."

In its most radical and most basic meaning, commitment to religious life means a consecration of one's total being, one's total self to Christ. Such a total giving of oneself to Christ is through and in a commitment to virginity. The

---

1. Vat. II, C. C., #45.

religious, vowed to virginity, does not stand with and beside a married partner, as one who is committed to the married state does. The religious, quite literally, frees himself from holding the hand of the one partner in marriage to whom one binds himself "till death do us part." Through virginity the religious binds himself in a special way to Christ.

Religious Life and Marriage:

To understand what commitment to religious life means, it is necessary to understand why, in marriage, the help of a sacrament, which effectively confers grace, is necessary. Christian marriage, because it is built upon and grows up out of the human, natural contract of marriage, needs to become a sign and a symbol of a higher reality, needs the help of Christ's effective grace to elevate it to a supernatural or God-orientated level. Not so the commitment to religious life. There is no sign or symbol of this kind needed. By the special grace attached to religious vocation, the one responding to this call is immediately linked with Christ. As Hans Urs von Balthasar writes: "The consecration of his (a religious) life makes of him a *sacrum* — i.e., he is given over the God, set apart for his sole use, a deputy (with Christ) for mankind, to be consumed for their benefit, for their reconciliation, a whole burnt offering."[2] Marriage, then, is a sacrament — a sign and symbol of Christ's love for us, his people; the religious life, a life of virginity, is not a sacrament, but is rather the actual reality of Christ's loving marriage for all eternity to his people.

Immediately, we can see some comparisons between a theology of marriage and a theology of the religious life. Both are to be based firmly on a foundation of love. Both

---

2. "A Theology of the Evangelical Counsels," **Cross Currents**, Spring, 1967, pp. 225-226.

loves, marriage and religious, are responses to a life of service — the former, to human service that becomes divine sacramentally; the latter to divine service that becomes incarnate through its special grace of consecrated commitment to virginity.

Is religious consecration in any sense a sign? Yes, Vatican Council II makes it very clear that it is.[3] But this does not make of it a sacrament as is marriage. The married state and the religious state branch out from a common source, the life of the Church, but contrast with one another. They do not by any means oppose each other, nor do they supersede each other. Rather, they stand in contrast to each other.

"The Better" Life:

A question poses itself immediately as to which of these two states of life is "the better." Traditionally, and more especially since the Council of Trent, the life of religious vows was designated as "the better." Today, in the light of Vatican II it is a bit difficult to state this as apodictically as formerly. Why? Since the reality is the same, and yet the structures by which this reality is known have changed, it is more difficult to situate the meaning of "the better."

First of all, every Christian is called to a life of perfection. Every Christian is called to respond with his *whole* being to love of God and love of neighbor. His response is the Christian commitment to the love option, as we have already seen. This, in itself, is "the better" way. In fact, this is the only way to Christian perfection, and even though a person can refuse this love option, by doing so and refusing this "love beyond," in a sense he loses what the Christian considers his all. But then, secondly, within the

---

3. Vat. II, C. C., #44.

entire framework of Christian perfection and holiness, God permits us to choose our own concrete and individual state of life. For the majority of Christians, the state of marriage, obviously, is the better choice. For them, marriage is very definitely the better means to lead a life of holiness. For them, marriage is "the better" way. On the other hand, God also offers a special grace, a special call to some Christians. It is not difficult at all to see that God does not call every Christian to religious life, though he does call every man to the Christian life. There is a difference here, the difference between a vocation common to all and a vocation call given only to some. In other words, the vocation to religious life does not depend merely on whether a person wants it or not. Religious vocation is a call, a grace given only to those who are capable of fulfilling that vocation and finding within it sufficient personal and Christian fulfillment.[4]

Finally, what an individual Christian chooses, with God's help and with all the human aids available to him, as his state in life, is always "the better" for him. After he has discerned God's vocation in the matter, what is chosen is "the better" means to perfection for him. This is what is usually meant by "the better," subjectively speaking. But what is objectively "the better" must be understood in the light of a mystery being revealed. Objectively, the religious life is "the better" state only relative to certain aspects of the mystery of God being revealed to us.

Such a call to religious life by God given to a particular person is not mandatory in the sense that refusal means aversion from God. In fact, it is held by many that one who does not have the desire or the resolution to accept this kind of life does not have a call at all.

---

4. Karl Rahner, S.J., "On the Evangelical Counsels," **Geist und Leben,** Würzburg, 37 (1964) 17-37.

Church As Mystery:

Constantly, it is necessary to recall to mind that the
Church is a mystery and that at no period or time of her
history can she exhaust fully the content of that mystery.
Different aspects of her life are either a sign of a deeper
reality or else make present here-and-now and reveal part
of that hidden mystery. We have already seen how this is
made possible through a sacramental life, especially in
relation to marriage as a state of life. Marriage as a sacrament signifies, in a way in which nothing else does, Christ's
present incarnational love for his Church, his people.

Religious life, the life of the counsels, manifests to us
another aspect of that mystery. Only with Vatican II did
the significance of this aspect of mystery become meaningful to us. "The profession of the evangelical counsels, then,
appears as a sign ... the People of God have no lasting
city here below, but look forward to one which is to come.
This being so, the religious life ... more adequately manifests to all believers the presence of heavenly goods already
possessed here below."[5]

This statement from Vatican II has to be explained
somewhat. The religious life cannot make manifest the same
aspect of the mystery of the Trinity as marriage does. This
should be obvious. Therefore, when the Fathers of the
Council speak of "the presence of heavenly goods already
possessed," they must be referring to the *eternal* Trinitarian
love for man.

This contrasts to the incarnational, present love of
Christ for his people witnessed to by marriage. In other
words, besides God's love for man in the present, existential
human condition, there is another aspect of God's love for
man — an unending, eternal love. Our temporal, human

5. Vat. II, C. C., #44.

condition has now been caught up into the eternal, Trinitarian love-life by Christ himself. This aspect of the mystery of God's eternal love for us becomes a revealed reality in and through religious life. This is "the sign" to which the Fathers of Vatican II refer.

Under the sign and symbol of religious life, God's eternal love for man in all man's humanness is made real for us in our present human condition. The commitment of the religious to this life is often expressed in terms more familiar to human marriage, and aptly so. In the religious state, a person binds himself by a special bond (a vow, oath, or promise) to Christ in such a way that the Divine Lover says with an eternal "I do" that God's love for man is both now and forever — an eternal, loving "I do."

Religious Life As Prophetic:

Once we understand this unique sign-value and revelation of the Trinitarian God-love that religious life is, only then can we penetrate to the basic meaning of the prophetic function of religious life in the Church. Every baptized Christian, every baptized member of the People of God, shares in Christ's priestly, kingly, and prophetic office.[6] At the same time, there is a variety of ministries in the Church. The Episcopate shares in these offices of Christ in a very special and unique way. By episcopal consecration alone is conferred the fullness of the sacrament of orders.[7] Through this sacramental consecration a permanent gift is conferred on men that involves the powers to sanctify, to teach, and to govern.

On the other hand, this same Council of the Church goes on to explain that,". . . the religious state constituted by the profession of the evangelical counsels does not belong

---

6. Vat. II, C. C., Chapter II, passim.
7. Vat. II, C. C., #21.

to the hierarchical structure of the Church."[8] Bishops are preachers of the faith, authentic teachers, speakers in the name of Christ, and infallible proclaimers of Christ's doctrine.[9] Obviously, then, the function and role of religious in the Church is not the same as that of the hierarchical Episcopate or the ministerial priesthood. We have to look elsewhere than to the hierarchical structure to find the specific function of religious life in the Church.

We have already seen that every baptized Christian shares in the priestly, kingly, and prophetic office of Christ. However, we must say that each shares in different ways, consonant with the function of his office. The layman, for instance, shares in the priesthood of Christ in an essentially different way from that of the ordained ministerial priest. The ministerial priesthood of a diocesan clergy, for example, does not partake of the prophetic or kingly office of Christ in the same way that the consecrated Episcopate does. We can ask, then, what function a Christian consecrated to religious life has to fulfill in the Church.

Something of an answer to this question was given by Vatican II in the *Constitution on the Church*. Perhaps the question was not posed in exactly these same terms, but the general direction of an answer can be found in Chapter VI of this decree. A number of items are mentioned in this chapter that are germane to the question at hand: the religious binds himself to honor and service under a new and special title; by such a profession he intends to free himself from obstacles that hold him from a greater fervor of charity; the bond is a better symbol of the unbreakable link between Christ and the Church; the religious life more adequately manifests the presence of heavenly goods already possessed; it foretells the resurrected state and the glory of the heavenly kingdom; it reveals in a unique way that the kingdom of

---

8. Vat. II, C. C., #44.
9. Vat. II, C. C., #25.

God is superior to all earthly consideration; it belongs in-
separably to the life and holiness of the Church. If we look
carefully at all these items expressing the unique nature and
function of religious life, two characteristics stand out: the
future reality present here and now, and the inseparable or
eternal love-link between man and God. These two characteristics make up the prophetic function of religious life
in the Church — the realized eschatology concerns a future
reality being lived out of faith, and secondly, a future
reality that is eternal being lived out in hope. Simply, eternal
love is being lived out in faith and hope.

Unique Prophetic Function:

If theologically this is the function of religious life in
the Church, then we should be able to express this even
more clearly since we have two thousand years of tradition
to look back to for evidence. This much can certainly be
said: the prophetic function of religious in the Church looks
to a constantly growing, constantly evolving, constantly
renovating reality. The prophetic thrust is to a future fulfillment. Nor is this the same as the prophetic function of the
episcopacy. The hierarchical Episcopate in its prophetic
role as teacher looks primarily to preserving the authentic
teaching of Christ, from the past historical event to the
present moment of salvation history. To preserve this de-
posit of revelation Christ willed that his Church be endowed
with the gift of infallibility. In matters of faith and morals,
the pope and the bishops proclaim Christ's doctrine infallibly.
At the same time, there is always in the Church a dynamism,
a thrust, a push, a drive that carries the Church from the
present into the future. It is in this future, this forward-
moving activity, that the religious should be unique. Not
that the Episcopate nor the laity play no part in this
prophetic role in the Church. Rather, we might say that the

religious life puts an ictus on the futurity of that prophetic role.

Historically, this has been the traditional role of religious. If we make a study of the founders of religious communities, for instance, the one element that stands out in almost every instance is the forward-looking, advanced thinking and activity of almost every one of them. Why were Anthony, Benedict, Bernard, Dominic, Teresa, Ignatius, Angela Merici, Francis de Sales, Mother Seton, and scores of other religious founders so outstanding? No one denies that they had great love in their hearts and rendered service to the People of God in an eminent way. But how? Their unique love was shown by their most evident forward-looking vision. They were concerned not merely with supplying service for present needs but even more with providing service for future needs with more daring love than usual. This was their "grace of office."

This very important, and almost unique, prophetic function of the religious has been either clouded or overlooked in recent years. Too many religious have been too concerned with bringing up to the present their past heritage. The preservation of the past and the guarding of tradition are both necessary and good. But what of their unique function of looking to "the world to come"— the future reality? The role of witness in the Church fulfilled by the religious is to show the world what is in store for it as a future reality; what the world has as its destiny. In a very awesome sense, the true "radical" in the Church should be the religious — always looking to the future reality. The religious by his very nature is a "radical" in the sense that he promotes the kingdom of God, which is the kingdom of peace, love, happiness and joy, a kingdom which the world alone cannot bring about. The grace of religious vocation makes it possible and necessary that this kind of "radical" witness is present constantly in the Church.

We can honestly and truthfully ask what has happened to this kind of witness in the Church. What has happened to religious life in the Church? Has there been a role-dif-fusion? Are religious more concerned about the security they find in a traditional pattern of life and not at all aware of or concerned about the risk that has to be taken constantly by those who are on the growing edge of a living, growing, developing Church?

In the context of prophetic vision in the Church, it is not too difficult to see why there are so many different kinds of religious communities. We have already seen the mystery-revealing function of the three major forms of religious life. From the viewpoint of prophetic vision, countless types of religious life have sprung up. This is good provided they serve a needed function in the living Church. Many different community-types have sprung up from the same basic spirituality, but all do not look forward to the same area of future evolution or development. Their apostolic thrust-areas are different.

More and more, we begin to see the specific and unique charism which is God's gift to religious. The unique charis-matic grace is not something connected directly with the hierarchical core of the Church. Should we not conclude that the charismatic grace of religious life is primarily a prophetic grace given to religious by and through the Holy Spirit? Should we conclude that it is through and in religious that the spirit of prophetism should be most evident in the Church?

Finally, in view of the uniqueness of the religious voca-tion as a prophetic charism, the importance for individual religious to be very conscious of a discernment of different spirits becomes evident. The religious needs some kind of guidelines by which he can judge how the Spirit (or spirits) is affecting him as an individual. More than anything, the love which is the basis of loving service, has to be a discern-ing love. There is also a very evident need for religious communities to discern the Spirit (or spirits) moving and urging members of the community who are functioning as "radicals." This response is obviously very closely connected with religious vocation, as we have seen. Since it is so much a part of religious life, religious communities should be most open to and most accepting of both superiors and members who live out, with all its uniqueness, their prophetic role as religious, no matter how "radical" that role may appear.[10] Religious should have not only an "open door" policy but an "open heart" policy — open in love especially to their own.

---

10. There has to be some distinction made here between being "radical" in the sense explained and being a "rebel." One can be a religious "radical" without ever revolting against authority. On the other hand, the primary characteristic of a "rebel" is opposition to legitimate authority and a corresponding insubordination. I am not hereby advocating within the Catholic Church a novel state of life of "religious rebels." I prefer to leave that novelty to others, more daring (?) than myself.

four

Religious in Community

The question of community and its meaning in religious life is certainly a number one problem today. Few Catholics, and even fewer religious, will disagree with the very acute statement of Father John Courtney Murray that there is a "crisis of community" in the Church today.[1] Some people still prefer to talk in terms of "crisis of obedience" or "crisis of celibacy" or even "crisis of identity." Once all these various crises in relationship to religious life have been examined, in the final analysis the crisis most evident is in the general area of community. This crisis is now out in the open.

Toward Definition:

If we are to talk about this crisis, it would seem that, first of all, there should be a definition of terms. In other words, what is the meaning of community in which there is a present crisis? To go to the dictionary and find a definition of community, and then to argue from such a definition, is futile. For instance, one of the first definitions of community in Webster's is a "a body of people having common organization of interests or living in the same place under the same laws." A good definition, for sure, but broad enough to include a community in a mental hospital. Or again, community can refer to an "assemblage of animals or plants." Obviously, a dictionary definition will be of little help.

---

1. "Freedom, Authority, Community," **America**, Dec. 3, 1966, p. 734.

Or we can go to another source of scholarship to find out what is meant by community. The great German scholar, Frederick Tonnies, even as far back as 1887, was distinguishing between "gemeinschaft-community" and "gesellschaft-society."[2] Tonnies described communities as closed, stable, coherent, and having warm human relationships. On the other hand, societies were open, mobile, functional, and having only transitory human relationships. He even made distinctions between primary and secondary groupings, between personal and ideological groupings, and so forth.

All in all, we do get an insight into the meaning of community from studies of this kind. But at the same time, one wonders whether the insight is not more into what the religious community is not, rather than what it really is.

Nor does it help the study of religious community, or the entire Church for that matter, to compare certain facets of the community with large corporations. Whether it can be shown by statistics that the Standard Oil Company is more efficient than the Church or not, does not give us too much insight into the real meaning of religious community. It can well be that a particular religious community is more efficient than, say, General Motors, and still not be a happy, joyful, meaningful religious community.

Part of the problem of trying to give a meaningful description or definition of religious community lies in the fact that we are so historically conditioned to use the human family as the analogue, the model for religious community. How often, for instance, is religious community compared, item for item, with the human family: need of father/authority figure, need of mother/loving figure, and need for children/obeying figure — all in harmony with one another. And often, the prime model, the prime living example of such a model religious community is the Holy Family.

---

2. Cf. "Making a Community out of a Parish," John de Witt, Cross Currents, Spring, 1966, pp. 197-211.

There is more to the problem than just that. Recently, like a tempest in boiling little teapot, a lot of steam has been raised as to the exact number needed to make up the perfect religious community. The controversy reminds one of the mystical numbers theory of St. Augustine that comes up periodically in one or other of the Third Nocturnes. Does three make the perfect community? It did for the Holy Family. Or is it twelve — like the Apostles? Or seventy-two, like the disciples? Or maybe thirty-three, the age of Christ when he died? All that this kind of thinking brings about is a greater problematic.

Toward Understanding Community:

This, then, is the question that faces us, the crisis of religious life: what is the meaning of community? It is not like the human family; it is not just another human business corporation; it is not determined by a set mystical number. What, then, is it?

In the first place, it is almost futile to start off with a definition or a clear and distinct idea of community. Starting off with such a concept is not too meaningful. Religious community, like the community of the Church, is part of the mystery of the Church. Community, like Church, is one of those fecund, deep, rich, and almost infinitely meaningful realities that all we can hope for is to get new and deeper insights into their true meaning.

In the second place, community is an analogous concept. There neither is, nor can ever be, a univocal definition of community. Community designates realities that are in some sense the same, and yet in other senses totally different. For instance, the human family is called a community. Religious community, too, has its uniqueness. Perhaps the prime example of religious community, that to which it can be compared most closely, is the Trinitarian community — all mature, equal, loving, free members; all co-equal and yet distinct. And yet, on the other hand, it is easily compared in some respects to the human family, and yet so infinitely different is religious community from it.

There are some characteristics common to all religious communities that can help us come to some understanding of its meaning. Certainly this much can be said, that every religious community gets its primary and original thrust through some kind of oneness in intention. Otherwise, all its members could be part of the community without having accepted religious life. The particular way in which this oneness of intention is expressed, the particular kind of external expression and external structure — both of which are necessary in a human community — will always depend on particular inspiration of the Holy Spirit. These inspirations come with the founding of a new religious group, with the setting up of the human institution corresponding to these inspirations, and finally, with the unique responses of those called to this state of life.

Creation of Community:

Equally evident with regard to religious life and community is the fact that the fullness of God's creative act is not exhausted at the original moment of the birth of a new religious community. Community is not fully nor completely realized at the original moment of creation. Neither the original founder nor any particular religious community exhausts fully the life of community. No moment of history can exhaust the full meaning of the mystery of community, nor can any moment of history make this mystery a finished reality. Community is a continuous creation. Community is a living, growing, on-going reality.

True, the original response and thrust of the founder of a particular religious community is important.[3] This should never be overlooked in any kind of renewal or adaptation. This original spirit is absolutely necessary, and to depart from this original thrust can only be verified if a new religious community is being founded. The original spirit of the founder is most essential.

But at the same time, in a particular moment of history, the uniqueness of a particular religious community has to be concretely realized. It is in a constant process of realization. For this reason it can be said that every religious community is in a constant state of creation. If there is one responsibility of a superior, and if there is one true response on the part of members of a community, it is that both are responsible that community be constantly and lovingly created. Community is not a static definition — like a rule. Community is not the founder or superior — like an individual person. Community is much more than all this.

Religious community, since it is situated in the Church and is part of that very life of holiness in the Church, must have many, if not all, of the characteristics of the Church as community. First of all, every religious is a member of the People of God. This means that every religious in community has an equality in dignity and freedom. Each has been called by the Spirit and has a common possession of that Spirit. Secondly, through Christ and in that same Spirit, all are united in a communion (*koinonia*). This communion through Christ and in the Spirit is the very basis

---

3. The meaning of community will have to be implied, most frequently from the context. At times it may be used in place of what has been often referred to as a religious institute. At other times it may refer to a part of the entire institute living together, as a local convent or even to a province.

of the religious interpersonal community. And thirdly, through the Spirit all religious have to respond to this interpersonal communion of love by service. This service rendered by religious results in a witness both by action that is performed — the work of the community — as well as by being something, by holiness — a living together in a community of free, mature Christians, the fullness of Christian life and of the perfection of charity.

The structure of community, therefore is going to differ with different forms of religious life as well as with different modes of service rendered by religious. It should be obvious, for instance, that certain things are proper to monastic religious community. A certain stability of one's whole life, not moving from place to place, greater stability in the order of one's day, more emphasis on the needs of the specific, immediate milieu of the community to which one has vowed himself — these are the specific characteristics of monastic religious life. For monastic religious, their community is their milieu. Characteristics of apostolic religious, on the other hand are: mobility, adaptability to broader needs of the Church than to the immediate milieu, sociability with all types of personalities and peoples, and so forth. For apostolic religious it is true that their community is their milieu, and their milieu is their community. Differences also exist in the specific orientations of secular religious toward the much broader community to which they are committed. For secular religious, as far as can be seen so far, their milieu is their community. One can almost say that in different ways and with different emphasis, every religious group is orientated and committed to creating community in a way peculiar to his own religious life commitment. We can even say, by analogy, that God has given to religious a power of cooperating in his creative act similar to a power he has given husband and wife.

Different Views of Community:

In contrast, there are often different views taken of religious community. For a very long period of time, for example, and this mostly because of pragmatic divisions introduced into Canon Law, community and common life meant almost the same thing. "In community" meant living in the same house, sharing the same food, following the same order, etc. Many items of common life, which should have been aids to creating community became real obstacles to community because of law and custom. A prime example in many communities was the recreation after meals, often required by a specific law. Whereas recreation together should have helped create better community, the law created tension for those who could not attend because of other work. The law caused division from those who could attend and felt that they alone were "obedient to the rule." Living the common life became identified with being a good religious.

Another view of community, taken perhaps more frequently today than ever before, is that the religious community is purely a functional entity. Regarded as functional reality, community gets its entire raison d'etre from the function its members perform — the work, the projects, the apostolate. Members in such a community are united merely by bonds of a common task to be performed — a group of students to be taught, a hospital to be conducted, a parish to be cared for, a social service to be rendered. The common task unites all into one community. Other things like housing, food, recreation, liturgy — all these are secondary and merely ancillary to the common task or apostolate.

The more that the mystery of religious community unfolds itself before us, the more we see that proper balance is required in all these areas. In other words, religious community must sustain its members spiritually, emotionally, socially, and intellectually. As a community of faith and love, real affective ties will have to be fostered among the members. As a visible community, some structure of authority will also be necessary. Some kind of balance will have to be reached between the individual in the community and the community as a whole. Call it common life or whatever name fits the reality, some kind of common bond also is needed. Moreover, every religious community, since it is a community of faith and love, has some kind of function to perform in Salvation History. This is the apostolate of the community, be it apostolic works or prayer. Thus, some kind of organization is necessary. This organization is necessary both for the sake of unity as in interpersonal community as well as for the sake of the apostolic action of the community. Thus it hinders insight into the real meaning of religious community to identify community with either "common life" or with "function." Religious community embraces both and yet more.

Prophetism and Religious Life:

As we have already seen, religious life by its very nature is committed to a prophetism of the future. Applied to community life, the religious should find in his community something pleasing to God, a situation in which he can find support for what he does — spiritual, psychological, and intellectual support. Living with others in community purifies one's own selfish tendencies; a structure of some kind of organization helps purify this selfishness also. At one and the same time, there is also a constant evolution taking place in view of the apostolic goal to be attained. There is an openness to change and the needs of the apostolate in spite of the common life structure that may be present. The structure of organization and the details of community life are desirable and valuable only in relation to the needs of the apostolic service to be rendered.[4] One wonders whether the primary witness of religious community in the Church today is not simply to live as a community of faith and love, but also to render service to mankind through its functional apostolate. In this light, not only is each individual religious by his commitment to vows living in a "realized eschatology," but also the entire community, big or small, is living out, in the present, a future reality — a realized communion of saints.

There are many, many conditions necessary for this kind of togetherness to be realized existentially. We are still in a human condition; we still live in an evolving universe; we still have our faults and limitations. Like the communion of all Christians, and the communion of saints too, the principal bond of any religious community is charity. Later on in the discussion of religious virginity, we will see how important human friendship is. But for the present let us emphasize that it is the virtue of love that holds primacy in binding religious together. This love has to be an interpersonal, realized love among consenting adults. In our human condition, and while our life is still being informed with faith and hope, other conditions are also necessary for healthy community.

Conditions for Good Community:

In the first place, there has to be *communication* between members, and this, both horizontally and vertically. It is not enough for members of a community to be on good

---

4. Again, it must be stressed that every religious community is committed to the apostolate of service to the Church. This apostolate may express itself in prayer, as it does for many monastic orders, or in apostolic works, as it does for apostolic religious. Both Xavier and Theresa were apostles; one of action and the other of prayer; one an apostolic religious, the other a monastic religious.

talking terms with each other. Nor is it enough for superiors
to say, "My door is always open." Communication between
members of a community and communication with the
superior are basic needs. Otherwise, there will be little
interest in the service being rendered and little possibility
of help or cooperation. Communication is not always in
words; sometimes our most meaningful communication is a
smile, a gesture, even only our presence. But some kind of
open communication there must be.

In the second place, since religious community is made
up of mature, consenting, open individuals, there is always
need of *consultation* for the good of the whole community.
Somehow every member should feel actively engaged in
community affairs. Such engagement is different for each
member of a community. But everyone should feel actively
engaged in the process of coordinating and promoting the
apostolate or in other things that directly affect the community. Even those who cannot work and spend their time in
prayer should be made to feel that they, too, are actively
participating in the life of the community. Consultation
should be open to all and not to a few and certainly not be
limited to a closed clique.

Thirdly, no human superior, no matter what his or her
gifts and native talents may be, can direct everything and
everyone within a community. *Delegation* of authority and
work is absolutely essential. Today, more so than ever, so
many talents, so many intellectual abilities, so many diverse
skills are needed for the well-run community that it is impossible for one person to possess all that is needed. The
superior today has to share responsibility. Based on a
principle of subsidiarity, this sharing of responsibility makes
it possible that problems are solved on the level at which
they exist. Superiors in communities should delegate authority and let others, better suited for particular jobs, assume
full responsibility. There should always be a margin allowed
for the making of mistakes. In other words, each one should

have the authority to solve the problems he is capable of solving.

Finally, a healthy, happy, and holy community will grow only if there is constant *cooperation* between all in the community. Call it what you will — team work, esprit de corps, community spirit, group witness — whatever name we use, it always comes down to the same reality. Cooperation within a community does not mean there are no tensions, no trials, no misunderstandings. We are still very human and still have to live in this human condition. But in spite of the limitations and the idiosyncrasies and the foibles, religious can still give witness to the world that they can live together in love.

It is very evident that some new structures will have to be introduced into many religious communities. All too few religious are familiar with methods of setting up committees. Few, if any, have taken part in group dynamic sessions. Most religious are more familiar with a notice on the bulletin board from a superior, than a call for a community meeting or a group discussion. These new structures have to become a part of religious life. Not only that, but superiors today have to show real interest and enthusiasm in introducing them. Otherwise, there may well be no real community witness given, and even worse, in time, no community to give witness at all.

Liturgical Community:

So many different factors enter into a discussion of religious life that it may tend to blur some of the most important of the traditional community responses. Today it is as true as it was yesterday that no matter what the form of religious life — be it monastic, apostolic, or secular — liturgical celebration is the heart of religious life. If it is true for the whole Church that "the liturgy is the summit toward which the activity of the Church is directed, at the same time it is the fountain from which all her power flows,"[5] then how much more true should this be of religious life which is committed to holiness? The prayer of every Christian has to be rooted in the prayer of the Church. The prayer of the Church finds full expression and flowers out into liturgical action. Within a religious community the celebration of the Eucharist is the very center of life. The Eucharistic celebration brings fraternal union to a perfection and makes it possible that God's blessing will be brought upon every apostolic endeavor or community project.

It is during the celebration of the Eucharist that religious confront in a face-to-face personal encounter their founder and superior, our Lord, Jesus Christ. With a togetherness not possible at any other time or during any other event of the day, Christ is present as priest, as prophet, and as superior. Gathered together about him this way, religious community is created in a unique way. *Communication,* even though not always verbal, is at a high point during the liturgy between superior and members, as well as between the members of a community who stand next to each other in loving witness. *Consultation* is at a high point here too, as all are asked to review and to pray for all the needs of the community and the needs of each other. *Delegation* is at a high point here, as all the members of the community perform the functions assigned to them in the celebration — even if it be only to say the prayers or to sing out, loudly and clearly. *Cooperation,* too, is at a peak because Christ himself is called to be present with all the community as all partake of his gift of himself to them.

Religious communities will have to give much more serious thought today than ever before to the place of liturgical celebration in their lives. They will have to realize that the climax of religious life is in the Eucharistic cele-

---

5. Vat. II, **Constitution on the Sacred Liturgy,** #10 (Hereafter designated as Vat. II, **C. S. L.**)

bration, rather than in some form of pious traditional community prayer. Even though it may be impossible for the entire community to be part of a common daily celebration, some provision will have to be made for periodic celebration — and in clerical communities, for concelebration — at which the entire community is present. Sub-communities, as for instance some members of one larger community all working on a specific project not common to the entire community, will have to realize their liturgical unity from time to time also. Communities active in parishes and schools must learn to participate more and more in the common parish liturgy and realize that they contribute a very important part to that liturgy. Only in these varied ways can religious come to understand that the Eucharistic celebration, and all liturgy for that matter, is both a cause of greater unity and love, as well as a sign or witness of unity and love.

Private Prayer in Community Life:

Not only the liturgical celebration but also the private prayer of a religious should have the same thrust. Every religious, and not just a select few, is called to a life of contemplation, whether that be contemplation in prayer or contemplation in action.[6] The religious, like every Christian, must also enter into his chamber to pray to the Father in secret.[7] Like all Christians, religious have to come to the liturgical celebration with the proper disposition, in order that their thoughts match their words, as Vatican II explains so well. Every religious, no matter how far advanced in the life of love, has to keep some time sacred, and leaving

---

6. In my division of religious life, I would place the traditional strict contemplatives under the form of monastic religious, whether men or women. Another use of strict contemplative will be explained in the final chapter.

7. Vat. II, C. S. L. #12.

all else aside, strive to find God, to experience God's presence in silent prayer. How often religious, and Christians for that matter, have deceived themselves into a situation that is bad logic and bad spiritual practice. To themselves they argue: all work is prayer; therefore, since I am so absorbed in apostolic work, my activity is my prayer. How false and how deceiving is this conclusion. The true "contemplative in action" is not one who has turned his whole life into activity, which he considers prayer. Rather, the true contemplative is one who keeps some time sacred for God, who strives to find God and encounter him in these sacred moments, who considers this daily dialogue with God truly vital activity of his day. Prayer "to the Father in secret" (Mt. 6/6) makes the action and the presence of God in the religious more increasingly evident.

Just as the liturgical celebration relates to community life, so should prayer relate both to the liturgical celebration and to the community life and apostolate. Through prayer a religious becomes a person for God and for others. But every one of us is different — our abilities, our needs, our work, our frustrations. Our individual and private prayer, unlike our common liturgical prayer, is a very personal, a very individual thing. Therefore, it is most vital that each religious seek out that manner and that kind of prayer which best aids him in finding God and conversing with God more intimately. Every person must find his or her own way to pray. Conferences, books, talks, methods — these all help. But finally, every person learns for himself.[8] The very first lesson that has to be learned by every religious is the fact that personal daily prayer is an absolute necessity.[9]

_____

8. Cf. "Prayer in Religious Life," Felix F. Cardegna, S.J., **Sacred Heart Messenger,** April, 1967, pp. 16-19.

9. Such is the insistence of the "Decree on Prayer" of the 31st General Congregation of the Society of Jesus, #11, p. 43.

Unity within Community:

For too long a time and too often we have stressed the differences that exist within religious communities. What can be considered an ecumenical movement has to take place within communities. In clerical communities, too much emphasis has been placed on the distinction between priests and brothers. Sisters stressed the differences between teaching sister and "lay" sister, or between mother and sister. In monastic communities, stress was put on the distinction between choir monk and lay monk. Today, in a post-Vatican II Church, religious have to realize that they are first and foremost religious; just that — religious. They have been given a vocation-call to religious life and have committed themselves to this state. Sisters, brothers, priests — all are religious and called to religious life in the Church. Their function within that religious life should be considered important but nonetheless secondary. Paragraph fifteen of the *Decree on the Appropriate Renewal of the Religious Life* states very clearly that the only difference that exists in communities is that which comes from the sacramental character of Holy Orders. Too many artificial distinctions have grown up in religious community life, and these distinctions often make the life of charity almost impossible.

five

Religious Chastity

That commitment to the religious life is one of only two vocation-options offered every Christian has been briefly discussed in an earlier chapter. Every Christian, as we have seen, is called to love; the particular way in which he responds is his own free commitment.

In marriage, two freely disposed persons commit themselves to each other, and decide freely to live with each other and to love each other in such a way that both are able to grow in love of God through each other. Now we ask: what of religious life? To what specific kind of love does a religious commit himself?

The Total Self:

No one will deny that commitment to the religious life is a commitment of the total self. This total commitment can be expressed in a variety of ways. Commitment to the religious life over the centuries has been expressed in multitudinous ways. Traditionally, however, the total commitment has been expressed most commonly by what are called the evangelical counsels, the three vows of chastity, poverty and obedience. In a sense, it is very secondary as to how man's total commitment to Christ is expressed. On the other hand, it would be foolish to ignore the many centuries of tradition through which the three vows have developed. Today, it may be better to talk more in terms of commitment to Christ, but it is almost impossible to do this in relation to religious life commitment unless we see the traditional meaning of the three vows. To ignore the meaning of the vows would be like ignoring the sacramental nature of marriage.[1]

Chastity and Christian Marriage:

The vow of religious chastity, which is the response of the Christian to the call to "celibacy for the sake of the kingdom of God," establishes the basis for the specific difference between religious life and the married state. It would seem that both biblically and theologically, religious chastity demarcates the difference between religious life and Christian marriage.[2] So much so that we can almost say that religious chastity has been a univocal concept in all of salvation history — yesterday, today, and the same forever. The concept of religious chastity does not change and has not changed over the centuries. Its meaning and essence are always the same. Similarly, it gives witness always to the same basic reality.

The same is not true of the other two vows, poverty and obedience. First of all, every Christian is called to a life of poverty and obedience. Christ made this very clear in the Sermon on the Mount. But not every Christian responds to poverty and obedience in exactly the same way. The response of married couples of obedience to each other

---

1. In the article by Hans urs von Balthasar mentioned previously, the following is stated: ". . . if talk about the 'three vows' is better omitted, since it obscures the existential value of the indivisible gift of self . . ." (p. 228). The traditional way of dividing this complete self-offering is into this three-fold division. Originally, the division was meant to avoid the very obscurity which some think it causes. The three vows express fully and comprehensively the gift of self. It is the self that is indivisible not the manner in which the self is offered.

2. The conclusions of Vatican II represent chastity as the sign of religious life much more so than either poverty or obedience. In Vat. II, C.C. #42, this is clear.

is quite different from the response to obedience, say of a Trappist monk. Yet, all are responding to Christian obedience. The same thing can be said of poverty: not all respond in the same way. In the second place, both poverty and obedience are analogous concepts. Both apply differently in different human situations. In fact, over the centuries there has been a real development of content with regard to these two vows and of the Christian response to them. This we shall study in later chapters. Not so with religious chastity. Its content and its meaning have remained the same, essentially, over the centuries. Just as the Christian sacramental marriage vow is essentially the same as it was in the early Church, so too is religious chastity.

Chastity in Scripture:

We can, in fact, go back even further than the New Testament to learn the meaning of religious chastity. Really though, the only true example in the Old Testament of "a celibate for the sake of the Kingdom of God" was the prophet Jeremiah. Even here, we find a relationship between his celibacy and the gift of prophecy. In the sixteenth chapter of *Jeremiah* we read:

> The word of Yahweh was addressed to me as follows: "You must not take a wife or have son or daughter in this place. For Yahweh says this regarding the sons and daughters to be born in this place, about the mothers who gave birth to them, and about the fathers who beget them in this land: They will die of deadly diseases, unlamented and unburied; they will be like dung spread on the ground; they will meet their end by sword and famine, and their corpses will be food for the birds of heaven and the beasts of earth."[3]

---

3. Jerusalem Bible, Jer. 16/1-5.

Notice that since Christ had not yet come, the loneliness of Jeremiah's virginal life looked forward to desolation: that of Israel. His was a prophecy of doom; his life of solitude foreshadowed the end of Israel. Jeremiah was living out a future reality, but it so happened that it was a future destruction.

In the New Testament, a new depth, a new meaning was given religious chastity by reason of the new revelation of Christ. St. Paul indicates this quite clearly in *I Cor.* 7. Even though Paul, mistakenly, considered the Parousia imminent and envisioned something much like the destruction of Israel as Jeremiah saw it, still very basically Paul understands religious chastity, that is "celibacy for the kingdom of God," exactly as Jeremiah did. The "unmarried for the sake of the kingdom of God" were prophets who told the world that the form of this present world is passing away.

Mary as Perfect Model:

Vatican II has given us a fresh insight into the meaning of the state of life option that may have been overlooked before. In Chapter 8 of the *Constitution on the Church,* the role of the Blessed Virgin Mary, Mother of God, in the mystery of the Church is presented in such a way that Mary, as both virgin and mother, is held out as the perfect model of the Church. Traditionally, certainly, Mary has always been the model of virginity and the model of the bride, of married life. Mary is both bride and virgin. She gives to all the world witness of perfect virginity and perfect motherhood. As the Mother of Jesus, she is a virgin; as Mother of the Church, in the words of Pope Paul, she is a virgin. Virgin-Mother best describes her as referring both to her relationship to Jesus and to his Church.

This relationship of Mary to the Church is by no means accidental. Noteworthy, too, is the great number of scriptural references that apply equally to Mary and to the Church.

Just as Mary was virgin and mother, as we have seen above, so the Church is both virgin and mother. Just as in Mary, virginity and motherhood were found in all their perfection and beauty, so in the Church, virginity and motherhood are found in their fullness.

We begin to see, more clearly and fully since Vatican II, how both virginity and marriage are needed in the Church for the revelation of the fullness of her mystery. Each — virginity and marriage — reveals different aspects of that profound mystery. Each has its own separate role to play that the mystery be revealed. In another sense, each needs the other to understand itself perfectly, and to understand its relationship to the mystery of the Church more perfectly.

Positive Meaning of Chastity:

The commitment to religious chastity, even though it is frequently described in a negative way as the "state in unmarried life," should be viewed in its true, positive meaning. Nor in a positive way should it be presented as the only perfect commitment to the love of Christ, since every Christian should respond in a total way to the love of Christ. In other words, not only those who have chosen religious chastity love Christ fully. Therefore, religious chastity has to be described in a positive way, and even though it will be impossible to describe adequately, since it is part of the mystery of the Church, still some positive things can be said about it that differentiate it from the love of the marriage-commitment.

First of all, whereas in marriage the partners commit themselves first and foremost to each other, and thus with the aid of a sacramental grace to Christ, in the vow of religious chastity, a person commits himself first and foremost to Christ, and thus also to the love of his fellow man. In the vow of religious chastity, no commitment is made to one, specific, individual human being exclusively as it is in marriage. If we use the imagery of marriage here, then we can say that the very essence of Christian virginity is a witness to the eternal marriage-love of Christ for all men. Religious life commitment "gives witness to all Christ's faithful of that wondrous marriage between the Church and Christ her only spouse, a union which has been established by God and will be fully manifested in the world to come."[4] The witness, then, is a fact of faith that the Church as a whole is a bride, wedded to Christ for all eternity with a virgin-love. The religious witnesses this eternal virginal love. The religious too, has to be very conscious of the true meaning of sacramental marriage as the religious life consists in a type of marriage relationship with Christ.

In the second place, religious life also gives witness to the fact that "God is." As we have seen, there is no natural counterpart for religious chastity. When a person commits himself to Christ by a vow of virginity, in the same act he is saying that life here on earth is not the whole story. He testifies by this act of faith that God is, God exists, God acts, God loves, even though we may not see or feel or touch or hear him here and now. As Cardinal Suhard once said: "To be a witness does not mean to spread propaganda, or even to create an impression, but to create a mystery. It means living in such a way that one's life would be inexplicable if God did not exist." The mystery proclaimed by religious chastity is the fact that God exists, and that the God who exists loves us.[5]

In the third place, the religious who is committed to chastity is not by that reason cut off from human love. Not by any means! A religious cannot be insensitive to love. A commitment to religious chastity is the commitment of a

---

4. Vat. II, A.R.R.L., #12.

5. For the ideas on "God is" I am heavily indebted to Father Cardegna who expressed the thought so very incisively in "Religious Celibacy," Sacred Heart Messenger, March, 1967, pp. 16-19.

human person, not of a mere thing. One can only be a full person when there is an "I-Thou" relationship established. In a very true sense, the religious by his vow of chastity, commits himself to establishing a community of love, not as a married couple does, but in a fuller, broader, deeper way. When we speak of a selfless love of neighbor and apply this to the commitment of religious life, then we mean that religious commit themselves to establish a community of love with any human person whom God chooses to send them. Obviously, this will be first and foremost the other members of their own religious community. But as we have seen, religious community can and does have a much broader scope. By this commitment through religious chastity to a community of love, religious give witness to an aspect of the mystery of the Trinity not found in any other facet of the Church. Religious, through their vow of virginity, make present here on earth a love-community which witnesses the Trinitarian love-community. Here is faith at one of its deepest levels because it proclaims to the world that a selfless love can be a reality here on earth because it is a reality in the Trinity. This community-love of the Trinity is an eternal love.

Renunciation and Chastity:

Only in the light of these positive aspects of religious chastity can the meaning of renunciation be understood. Frequently, renunciation of the religious life is expressed in terms of "denial of all sex activity." To express renunciation in these terms, and only in this way, is to make the same mistake as to express marital love completely in terms of physical sex. Both would be misleading.

A religious with a vow of chastity should, ideally, like a married person, possess a pure and perfect human love. This love should encompass both spiritual and emotional love. Renunciation of marriage for the religious does not, by reason of the vows, stunt that pure and perfect love. We can't conclude to this any more than we can conclude that since married partners do not take religious vows that therefore they stunt their pure and perfect love for each other.

Renunciation for the religious does not mean renouncing love, or affection, or even human friendship. Much less does it mean denouncing sex as evil. It does mean renouncing the physical procreative act and all its attendant sexual pleasures. But just as marriage does not find its fullest and deepest meaning in the merely physical procreative act and its pleasures, neither does the religious commitment find its full meaning in the renunciation of this aspect of love. Rather, its deepest and fullest meaning is found in the total, unconditional love and dedication to the service of Christ. Thus, we can conclude that renunciation for the religious who takes a vow of chastity means renouncing the procreative function, the deliberate sexual pleasure that accompanies it, and the affection connected with married love and family life. However, even though the religious renounces these, he does not repress these natural urges and turn them into complexes. If there is question here of sublimation, the only urges sublimated are the physical, sexual responses. The mature religious sees true value in what he is renouncing, but he sacrifices them out of love.

Maturity and Chastity:

Why must this be true? For a religious who is committed to chastity, the same degree of maturity is required as for any Christian who wishes to be committed to a perpetual vow in marriage. If a man and woman are going to commit themselves to each other in marriage — and this perpetually — it is necessary that they have developed, before they marry, an unselfish, mature love for each other. Unless there is a mature, unselfish love one for the other before marriage, then the mere expression of physical love after marriage will not make that love mature. Existentially the procreative act is the expression of a love already developed, already mature, already unselfish. If it is not that, then it is not an act of a human person, and therefore, not an expression of love.

Unless we admit that a person must come to making a commitment — either to religious life or to marriage — as a mature, fully developed human being, then we are going to find ourselves in some rather dangerous predicaments. One such predicament results from the statement that for perfect and complete personality, for full maturity, and for healthy affective relationships with other persons, one needs the complementary perfecting value of the opposite sex. This is usually expressed as the philosophy of complementarity. It is usually situated in and explained as the theory of the depth psychologist, C. G. Jung. He looked upon the soul as bi-sexual, containing functions he labeled "animus"and "anima." Masculine and feminine were determined by which of these —"animus" or "anima"— was conscious and which unconscious. Only a member of the opposite sex could awaken, activate, and bring into peaceful relationship the unconscious element. At times this theory is presented in more sophisticated, Teilhardian terms.

What happens when this theory is applied unconditionally to a person committed to religious vows? The obvious conclusion is that a religious — man or woman — would need a member of the opposite sex to attain full personality development and therefore, even perfection or sanctity. Obviously, such a view goes contrary to the conclusions of Vatican II, that "the profession of evangelical counsels, though entailing the renunciation of certain values which undoubtedly merit high esteem, does not detract from a genuine development of the human person."[6] It is very highly improbable that Vatican II was proposing a "third way," by which men and women religious could commit

6. Vat. II, C.C. #46.

themselves to each other and still be committed first and foremost to Christ.[7] Carl Jung notwithstanding, such a "third way" is a religious anomaly.

Normally, full personality development should have taken place before one finally decides to accept commitment to a perpetual vow, whether that vow is the "yes" to married life or to religious life. Ordinarily, this would mean that one's emotional and affective life should be sufficiently developed before such a commitment takes place. True, after commitment takes place, there is always room for more development. Nor can every religious expect this development to take place in complete isolation from the other half of the human family. This further development, which consists in a more harmonious integration of one's affections and emotions, of one's whole person, may even involve a mature religious, in some instances, in close personal relationships with members of the other sex. These close relationships can be a real good for a religious, provided a degree of maturity has already been attained which can sustain them. Such relationships have always to be conditioned by one's vow of chastity as well as by the personal identity of each person involved.

Even a fully mature religious, face to face with this kind of close personal relationship with a person of the opposite sex, runs a risk. There is always the danger that physical love will express itself in exactly the same way it is expressed in marriage. Or again, the emotional absorption between two religious can develop into an exclusiveness that is more proper to pre-marital love. Such absorption in each

---

7. Some examples of articles that lend themselves somewhat to an ambiguity if interpreted in this way are: (1) "Complementarity: Man and Woman, Marriage and Virginity," David B. Burrell, C.S.C., **Review for Religious**, Jan. 1967, pp. 149-160; (2) "Teilhard, Sexual Love and Celibacy," Charles W. Freible, S.J., **Review for Religious**, March, 1967, pp. 282-294; (3) "Sexuality and Emotional Maturity," Eugene Kennedy, M.M., **The Critic**, April-May, 1967, pp. 15-19.

other impedes, for religious, their psychological and spiritual growth. An even more subtle danger is that one person uses another as a "thing," for the self-fulfillment and self-gratification of psychological needs that have been suppressed or lurk beneath the level of one's consciousness.

A fully mature religious will face these relationships with an open mind and at the same time see the great need for discernment, for an understanding of the psychological aspects of such a relationship, and for open communication with an advisor. With a mind and heart open to all these influences, a mature religious can discern whether peace is present or not within himself, in this relationship, and with God. Such discernment, however, is possible only if a person is mature. It should not be too difficult to see that committing oneself to religious vows with an immature personality can be as disastrous to a person as coming to married life, and living in the married state, immaturely. Little wonder that so much emphasis is being put today on mature and responsible personalities, as they alone are capable of making permanent commitments.

Nor does the answer for religious lie in taking a negative attitude toward the world, and toward sex in particular. The attitude of fleeing "the world" into the safe ghetto of a religious community is not going to solve any problems.[8] To look upon the world, one's body, and sex as the sources of evil in life will create even more problems than it is intended to solve. To denigrate marriage and physical sex in order to extol religious vows, and to conclude that religious life is "the better" because of this reason, is not good psychology, much less good theology, and even less true charity.

---

8. Similar conclusions were reached in the "Recommendations of the Santa Clara Conference for Jesuits. Cf. **Change Not Changes: New Directions in Religious Life & Priesthood**, C. J. McNaspy, S.J., Paulist, 1968.

Friendship and Chastity:

We often hear that the basis of a good religious life is charity. The "primacy of charity" has been proposed over and again of late as the most fundamental aspect of religious life, and of all Christian life for that matter. If we examine the matter conceptually first, and then existentially, I wonder whether our conclusions would be as simple as that. It is evident that the now-famous "hippies" have made love the basis of their lives and of what limited activity they are involved in. Their "love-ins" are only too well known. Yet, for all the goodness that may be in their hearts and in their activity, one wonders whether this is the whole picture. Is life just one big "love-in"?

If we stand apart from religious life and look at it conceptually, it would seem that the basis of this state of life option, which is also a commitment to community, is friendship. Looking at human nature in "the raw" so to speak, we find that all men have some rather strong impulses which we call emotions. No matter how we list them or number them, the emotions of fear, anger, hope, joy, hate, love, and so forth, are very evident. Men experience these responses which are primarily psychological but also have strong physical repercussions associated with them. Man as man also has a knowledge of himself which is conceived of as a self-possession, a presence to self, as well as a deep desire for self-realization, which is conceived of as self-actuation. To attain the fullness of his being, man desires freely to dispose himself in loving communication with another human as a "Thou." This communication which involves the knowing "I" and a free self-disposition, along with the emotional experiences aroused, is the very heart of human friendship. Not only the emotion of love is involved. Rather, the whole being, human in every way, desires to establish a loving communication with the "Thou." From this primary and basic human communication, a full and rich "I-Thou" encounter follows, and human friendship has been born. Even though such an encounter may be established in a "grace-atmosphere" and may be informed by the presence of a divine Love, still all the human elements must be present. One can accept or reject an individual "Thou" in such an encounter. On the basis of acceptance one grows in friendship (or one rejects and grows in hate).

Friendship, the result of accepting "I-Thou" encounters with one's fellow men, is the natural milieu in which charity, a supernatural reality, can grow.[9] Man cannot dispose himself for loving communication with "the other" unless "the other" is first of all known. No one can truly love as a person something that is not first known. Thus, loving communication starts on a very basic and very existential human level — the level of what we usually call friendship.

Little wonder, then, that the very same basis has to be established for religious life. Just as loving communication starts with friendship — an expression of my full being, emotions included toward "the other"— so also is a loving communication the basis of religious life, established in the very same way. If this is true, then it should be evident that the response to religious chastity is not something apart from real, existential life. Quite the contrary! In every way it can be said that commitment to the vow of chastity is a commitment to a full and complete love, both of God and of neighbor. In fact, the very same human affections and emotions needed for a healthy human married life are also needed for a healthy and happy religious community life.

Meaning of Universal Love:

There is a real fallacy often expressed when the idea of the religious commitment to universal love is explained.

---

9. Vat. II, **A.R.R.L.** #2 and #18. In fact, religious today have to be more attuned than ever to that world in which they are giving Christ-like service out of love.

A commitment to "love all" does not mean that, as a religious, I am bound to love everyone, universally, and in exactly the same way. Such an explanation is a parody of love and friendship. To "love all" in exactly the same way would mean to ignore the uniqueness and the individuality of "the other." To "love all" in this way would mean to go out to "the other" as an "It" rather than as a "Thou." Thus, a pure, emotionless, "spiritual" love, which loves all in exactly the same way, is really not love at all. The religious, committed to chastity, is committed also to universal love, but it is a universal love that is still within the framework of human nature. We are not angels nor are we God. As humans, religious are endowed with the same human feelings, emotions, and affections that every other human is. They must use these in establishing true and intimate human friendships, preciously few though they may be. The human affection here must be genuine; the love must be real. "These human loves are perfectly compatible with the total and immediate love of God to which the religious has consecrated his life."[10]

Loneliness in Life:

Only in the light of friendship as a loving communication and the religious life as a community of love can the whole notion of loneliness in religious life be understood. Loneliness is not caused by man's commitment to a life of religious chastity. Nor is loneliness the same as "aloneness." In the world today, in spite of the large cities and in spite of the crowds, man is often still very lonely. Loneliness seems greatest in crowds! Loneliness is the result of lack of communication or an inability to encounter another in an "I-Thou" relationship. Should we say, even, that loneliness is the absence of friendship? The religious who experiences loneliness,

---

10. Cf. "The Unity of Love of God and Love of Neighbor," Karl Rahner, S.J., Theology Digest, Summer, 1967, pp. 90-91.

like any other human being with the same experience, has a psychological problem that grows out of a human condition and not necessarily out of a religious vow. A lonely person communicates with no one or with a few, poorly. Often, a lonely person is incapable of real, existential communication and may even feel no need for it.[11]

"Aloneness" and solitude are quite different from loneliness. It may well be that modern man feels his loneliness so intimately at times for the simple reason that he cannot withdraw from the crowd or because he is afraid of his own "aloneness." Without friendship and without a healthy "I-Thou" encounter with his fellow man, it is impossible for him to establish any fuller or deeper relationship with a "Thou" who is God. Really, the latter depends on the former.[12]

A religious on the other hand, committed to religious chastity, has at least the basis for rich human and divine love in friendship and in all the affections that surround such friendship. With a firm basis of friendship in life, the religious should not be afraid either to extend himself in service to the community — whether it be the limited religious community or the fuller People of God — nor to withdraw and in solitude to be alone with God. The very fact of having healthy "I-Thou" encounters with his fellow man makes it both possible and meaningful to experience the "I-Thou" relationship with God. Thus, and only thus, does one love lead to "an-Other" Love.

---

11. "Perfect Chastity and Human Affectivity," Felix F. Cardegna, S.J., **Review for Religious**, May, 1964, pp. 309-315. (In this article is also treated the topic of particular friendships.)

12. For an adequate treatment of friendship see **The Ways of Friendship,** Ignace Lepp. His chapter on "Friendship and Loneliness" is a more penetrating treatment of what I have been trying to express in relation to religious life.

SIX

Religious Poverty

Earlier it was stated that religious chastity is and has always been a univocal concept — always the same — whereas both poverty and obedience, because of development and change and differences, must be considered as analogous concepts. This is certainly most evident today in a discussion of poverty. Especially in a society which is affluent and yet must declare a "war on poverty," obviously religious poverty and the "war on poverty" must mean radically different things. Yet, we do use the word poverty for both. Our attempt to understand poverty as an analogous concept must take us back to a study of biblical poverty first of all.

"The Poor" of Biblical Revelation:

Even in the Old Testament no one word adequately expressed the idea of "the poor" as we use the word today.[1] Words such as *'anî, 'anaw, dal* and *'ebyon,* all have nuances and shades of difference that vary in meaning, from indicating membership in a lower class of people to the properly poor and needy. Another nuance of "the poor" is found particularly in the *Psalms.* Here, "the poor" takes on a more religious tone and signifies one who is religious minded, or what we might call holy. Both the *Psalms* and *Isaiah* identify Judaic piety and holiness both with "the poor" and with an absence of social standing. The "rich"— the wealthy and

---

1. "Poor; Poverty," **Dictionary of the Bible**, J. McKenzie, S.J.

those having social standing — are posed in opposition to "the poor"— the needy and the lowly. Destitution, to the Hebrew, seemed to point up and reveal the sins of the proud and of the rich, who lacked a proper attitude toward poverty. A few of the *Psalms*, such as 9-10, 34, and 37, perhaps best of all, indicate how the good man should feel toward poverty. Such a man is posed as one who is very familiar with suffering in life and yet, at the same time is certain that God is constantly with him. He knows peace and joy because God is always with him. It is rather evident in the Old Testament that an attitude of mind best epitomizes the basic stance of "the poor" rather than a mere identification with the destitute and the depressed.

The word *'anaw*, used to designate the attitude of Moses in *Num.* 12/3, is the same word used by Christ to designate "the poor" of the New Testament.[2] When one is confronted with texts such as the Sermon on the Mount of *Mt.* 5/3 and *Lk.* 6/20, he sees that the revolutionary thrust injected by Christ is that even "the poor" will enter the kingdom of heaven. He sees further that "the poor" here are those who have not found peace in a prosperous life but in the riches of a friendship with God. As used here, "the poor" is placed in sharp contrast to the "rich" Pharisee.

Yet, nowhere in the New Testament does the meaning of "the poor" stand out so clearly and fully as in the life of Christ himself. He was a poor man himself and chose to be a friend of the poor. Christ's idea of "the poor" is brought out most clearly by St. Paul in 2 *Cor.* 8/9. When Paul says that Christ though rich became poor for the sake of men, he is obviously referring to more than material riches. The poverty of Christ is best characterized by his renunciation of his privilege as Son of God and his choice of a human

---

2. The **Jerusalem Bible** translates: "Now Moses was the most humble of men, the humblest man on earth."

condition with all the inherent limitations this meant. Christ, too, had the choice of fundamental option. And this, even to death, which was part of that human condition. Thus, choosing to be extremely poor — namely, our human condition in contrast to the divine condition — he showed men extreme riches: the divine condition to which we are called.

Only in this context of Christ's free choice of a "poor" human condition can we understand how poverty is a condition of life to which every Christian is called. Poverty is part and parcel of the Christian dynamic. Without the same poverty response to which Christ himself responded, there is no true Christian response at all. In other words, to be Christian means to be poor.

Only when we understand Christ's free choice to be poor can we understand the meaning of the "Church of the poor" as used by Vatican II. In the first chapter of the *Constitution on the Church,* the Church is presented as a poor Church, a pilgrim Church, a Church that shares the same poverty and suffering as Christ, its founder. If the true Church of Christ is the "Church of the poor," then in some sense every Christian must share in the same poverty in which Christ shared.

The Christian "Poor":

What, then, is this Christian poverty to which every Christian has been called and to which every Christian must respond if he is ready to be a Christian? Two things Christian poverty is not. First, the call to Christian poverty is not a call to destitution. Christ did not identify "the poor" with the destitute; this is not at all the meaning of the beatitude. Destitution in a real sense is privation of a need; it is an evil. Even though a Christian should show sympathy toward the destitute, no Christian should look upon destitution as a good in itself or a good for the kingdom of God.

This is a perversion of the Christian good news. And second-ly, evangelical poverty should not be identified with a col-lective sharing of property and material goods, although collective sharing may be a legitimate and extended applica-tion of the Christian message. But it does not constitute the Christian commitment to poverty.[3]

As conceived by Christ, as chosen by Christ, and as lived by Christ, poverty was not an end in itself. Nor should it be for the Christian. Basically, to be poor for the Christian means to be willing to divest oneself of all things here on earth in order to obtain the riches of God. For the Christian who is poor, the riches of divine life are always placed above and considered superior to whatever riches this world can offer. For the Christian, as for Christ, poverty is associated with some form of abandonment of oneself, a renunciation of one's own privileges or position or power for the sake of the kingdom of heaven. Thus, for the Christian, true poverty means to be completely and fully committed to Christ, who is our eternal treasure.

Once again, it becomes evident that Christian poverty is basically an attitude, a disposition, a commitment that is Christ-orientated. It may mean in some instances not only the use of, but the possession of, many material things. It may mean, and often does mean, the development and use of one's own native riches — abilities, talents, and personality qualities. But all this is for the interest of the kingdom of God. However, Christian poverty may also mean at times and for some a real sacrifice of comfort, of material posses-sions, of enjoyments, and even of the use and development of one's own talents. But again, this is all meaningless unless it is for the kingdom of God.

---

3. For a development of this topic see, "Evangelical Poverty," Jean Danielou, S.J., **Cross Currents**, Summer, 1959, pp. 379-388.

"The Poor" in Religious Life:

Unless the vow of religious poverty is seen against this traditional Christian background, it can become an utterly confusing commitment. The use of material goods, personal possessions, native abilities and talents, yes, and even time, has to be first of all situated in the context of the Christian commitment. Then, and only then, does the specific commitment of a religious vow have meaning.

Since all Christians are committed to poverty by the very fact of their response to Christ, religious by their vow merely make more specific this Christian commitment. In other words, a religious vow of poverty merely specifies this more general Christian commitment. For this reason, the religious vow of poverty can vary tremendously from one religious community to another. Religious commitment to poverty can vary all the way from a vow to live a life of near destitution, and so to be able to identify more closely with the neediest of the needy, or to what is merely a re-affirmation of the general Christian commitment, as it is in some secular institutes. The specific way in which a religious disposes his possessions to poverty can, therefore, vary through a whole gamut of forms, partly like and a great deal different from each other. But, at the same time, no one form completely exhausts the meaning of or the expression of Christian poverty. One's apostolic work may demand one form; another's apostolic milieu may demand another form. This, and this alone, is what makes one form better than another.

Even though the religious vow of poverty is not determined or constituted by its witness value, yet the witness value of poverty must be an active consideration in any specific form of community observance of poverty. Most religious will agree with the concepts and the principles that form the basis of a vow of poverty. But in the specific applications of a vow, some religious either fail to see the meaning of the vow or they simply fail to observe the vow. Witness can follow only from a poverty actually lived out in reality. If members of a community should be practicing a specific form of poverty by rule, but no one in the community is observing this practice, it is hardly possible that a Christian witness will follow. If, for example, one's rule calls for turning in gifts, getting proper permissions for the use of money, and getting along without unnecessary conveniences, but no one in a community does any of these, how can religious witness follow?

Even after the Council of Trent's trenchant study of the meaning of religious poverty, religious life is still cursed with the problem of the independent *peculium*. Today, the forms and uses of the *peculium* may be quite different from what they were in years gone by, but the problem is the same. Whether the *peculium* takes the form of private financial gifts from relatives and personal friends, or use of facilities belonging to friends such as cars, boats, equipment of all kinds, credit cards, and even living quarters, or the possession of private funds apart from the community, the same problem of *peculium* exists: Religious in the community are divided into the "haves" and the "have nots." The perennial response that a gift offered from a private source costs the community nothing merely aggravates the problem because religious today should more easily see the fallacy of this sophistry. If poverty, in whatever form, is to be the "firm wall of religion" it should be, it is yielding to sophistry of this kind that will weaken the ramparts. Not only is Christian witness to poverty not given, but a deep destruction becomes inevitable: A most serious wound is inflicted on community morale.

No matter what the specific form, if members of a religious community are able to be sufficiently detached from themselves and their possessions and at the same time sufficiently attached to Christ, witness to religious poverty will always follow. But one thing is most important: One has to be sufficiently attached to Christ, already experiencing the life of the kingdom, already realizing the goodness and the gifts of God in his life before he can give any kind of witness. Being destitute, foregoing pleasures, giving up one's possessions – all these things are negative and in a sense meaningless to a religious unless he is already living the Christ-life and experiencing the kingdom of God in his heart. This is what the phrase "becoming poor with the riches of Christ" really means.[4]

Dependence and Work:

Over the course of centuries, the vow of poverty for religious came to mean, for the most part, some form or other of dependence. One of the most traditional forms has been living on alms. It became quite evident, even before Vatican II, that in many instances religious who had taken vows to live on alms could no longer live this way and still give true Christian witness. Such radical social change had taken place in the world that new forms for expressing religious poverty had to be found so that witness could have meaning in the world today. The Fathers of Vatican II made every effort to return to more traditional forms of poverty and to emphasize more the biblical concept of poverty. In the Decree on *Appropriate Renewal of the Religious Life,* Number 13, this idea is brought out very clearly.[5]

---

4. In the article "Poverty in Religious Life," Ladislaus M. Orsy, S.J., (Review for Religious, Jan. 1967, pp. 67-69) spells out in concrete terms the full meaning of the "riches of God."

5. An excellent analysis of the decree, and one of the few written so far, is "Commentary on the Decree on the Renewal of Religious Life," Paul Molinari, S.J., Supplement to: The Way, May 1966. For matter on poverty, pp. 44-49.

In this decree it is clearly stated that mere dependence on superiors for material things does not constitute the full meaning of religious poverty. Once again emphasis is placed on the supernatural principle of faith, the commitment to Christ, and the following of Christ's example. One has to have this personal, dynamic, living experience of the gift of Christ before the sacrifice of man's few human possessions by a vow of poverty has any real meaning. Nor is the decree remiss in giving a very practical, down-to-earth and effective way to live out one's religious vow of poverty. Very simply Vatican II says that like all humanly poor men, religious also should work for their living.

Working for one's living might sound like a very simple idea. It is. That is why it can be said that Vatican II has made it possible to strip away all the unnecessary embellishments that have been really hiding the true biblical meaning of poverty. Sharing in the poverty of Christ (*Mt.* 8/20); storing up treasures in heaven and not on earth (*Mt.* 6/20); working for one's living but still putting all confidence in our heavenly Father (*Mt.* 6/25); real effective and affective love for the poor (*Mt.* 19/21), even to renouncing one's own inheritance to identify better with the poor — these are the biblical expressions of poverty offered to religious for imitation.

By the vow of poverty a religious gives witness to all men that everything he is, everything he has, everything he possesses is from God — God's gifts to him — which he now stands ready to share with all men. He possesses nothing as his own, and what he has, he freely gives to others. Through his vow of poverty he lets men know that not only he himself but all that he possesses are directed to and of service to "the other." He works and develops all the talents and abilities God has given him. What remuneration he gets — whether it be monetary or developed talents — all this he gives back to men as gifts from God.

A Theology of Work:

For the religious, a theology of work has to be very closely linked to the theology of the vow of poverty. For every Christian, work must be looked upon not as an evil or as a punishment for sin, but rather as the means God has given man to imitate him by putting order into chaos. Only pain and suffering as frequent concomitants to hard work are the curses of sin. Through work, every Christian must realize that he continues to create the world with God by making it a better place to live in and helps bring it into a more finished state. St. Paul addressed his remarks to all Christians when he wrote: "For creation was condemned to a futile existence, not willingly, but by the will of him who doomed it. Yet hope still remained that even creation itself would be delivered from its slavery to corruption and would come to share in the glorious liberty of the children of God." (Rom. 8/19-20). Man's work not only helps create the world, but creates society, community, and even helps God create man himself. Pope Paul states this very clearly: "God who has endowed man with intelligence, imagination and sensitivity, has also given him the means of completing his work in a certain way."[6]

The Christian brings even more than this to his work. Through his faith and belief in the Incarnation, the Christian also believes he brings a redemptive action to his work. With a belief in his union with Christ, the Christian believes that his ordinary work can and does become a liturgy of action, in, with and through Christ. The Christian believes he helps redeem the world, society, and man himself through his loving action, his work.[7]

---

6. Paul, Dev. Peop., #27.

7. One of the finest summaries of a Christian theology of work is found in Teilhard's The Divine Milieu, "The Divinisation of Our Activities," especially part 5, A, in which the sanctification of human endeavor is discussed.

The religious with a vow of poverty comes to his work which is already impregnated with a very rich Christian significance. He comes to work not as to something that is an evil in itself, nor as something that merely promises money, pleasure, and power or that invites one to greater and greater selfishness. The religious, like every Christian, comes to his work with a sense of duty, a professional awareness, a realization of a mission of sharing in the creation of a supernatural world that still remains incomplete.[8]

This, then, must be the attitude of a religious toward work if he is to understand why the Fathers of Vatican II linked work with the religious vow of poverty. If work is merely looked upon as an evil to be borne with, as a suffering to be undergone, as an ascetical practice which may or may not be practiced, then it will be almost impossible to see how it can be linked so intimately with a vow. If work is only a curse to be suffered through, and it is thus linked with the vow of poverty, then Vatican II can be charged with giving only a negative insight into the vow. On the other hand, if work is looked upon as creative, redemptive, and as an aid to creating community by uniting wills, minds, and hearts of men, then the thrust of the vow of poverty is very positive, very meaningful.

If man works, obviously he will enjoy the fruit or the wages of his work. But what of the religious who must consider work as an expression of his poverty? Must he shun the fruits of his industry? Should the modern religious, like the monk of old, "pull apart at night all the baskets he wove during the day lest he become proud."[9] In religious life today this has become a very serious question. The "wages for work" of religious have in very many instances

---

8. Paul, **Dev. Peop.**, #28.
9. "Is It Basket Weaving?" **We Hold These Truths**, J. C. Murray, S.J., pp. 175-196.

become enormous — they possess large and very modern schools, well-equipped hospitals, most impressive community houses, functional parish plants. Not only this, but religious have become thoroughly engrossed in expensive and elaborate courses of studies, acquire impressive academic degrees and status. As students of culture, they travel a lot, and even when necessary develop private libraries. One can be seriously tempted to ask, quite frankly: Is religious poverty fact or fiction?[10]

The solution to this complicated problem is not simple. On the other hand, the approach to such a problem should not be simplistic. The problem here with regard to religious poverty is basically the same problem as the use of creatures for any Christian. As Teilhard acutely observes: "One thus evades the basic problem of the use of creatures if one solves it by saying that in all cases the *least possible* should be taken from them."[11]

The answer obviously is not found simply in a non-use of the creatures, especially not in our modern, affluent society. Nor is it found simply in the least possible use of such creatures. Nor will the answer be found merely in stating that religious should not be taking a vow of poverty because the observance of poverty is so very ambiguous today. If anything, the ambiguity lies not in the observance of religious poverty but in the very use of the word poverty in an expression like: "War on Poverty." It should read rather: "War on Destitution"— for that is what it is.

To avoid use of modern creatures — even multi-million dollar plants — to change names for appearance's sake, to be overly consious of witness value rather than true inner

---

10. Such a question has already been asked: "Religious Poverty: Fact or Fiction?" Eugene Ahern, S.J., America, May 20, 1967, pp. 753-4.

11. "Some General Remarks on Christian Asceticism," The Divine Milieu, part C.

meaning, to concentrate on external appearances of poverty
rather than its inner dynamic, to avoid risks because of the
danger of losing "sign value"— these are all the temptations
that religious can fall into unless the religious vow of poverty
is seen as a very substantial part of the Christian dynamic.

The only theological avenue that is open in a full and
broad perspective is the way opened to us by Christ himself.
The poor religious is the person who possesses and is possessed by God. He is poor because he knows that everything
he is and has and possesses have been given him by God
as gifts, and he freely wishes to use them and to give them to
others in a spirit of loving service. His religious vow of
poverty merely specifies this more concretely.

For all these reasons, and more, there have been and
are different expressions of religious poverty. For some,
religious poverty is specified as using a modest little house
all by oneself and using one's time in contemplation. For
others, it means having no stable home, no money, no bank
account, no insurance for the future. For some, religious
poverty may mean using modern, expensive, well-furnished
living and working facilities for their apostolic work. For
some religious, time will be used for silence and prayer;
for others, time has to be used in loving and needed converse with others.

Religious poverty, it must be insisted, is an analogous
concept. For all it is the true and full imitation of Christ;
thus it is the same for all religious. As a specific, concrete,
existential expression, however, it varies infinitely. To say
that religious poverty should be the same for all, or to identify
religious poverty with destitution is to run the risk of losing
all, both the spirit and the fact of poverty. Ragged clothes,
poor food, run-down houses, poor equipment — these are not
necessarily signs of religious poverty. They may well give
witness to laziness as to anything else.

Individual Religious Poverty:

It should not be too difficult to see that just as different religious communities specify the observance of poverty differently, so also religious poverty will be observed by individuals, even within one community, differently. Why? Because as it has been shown repeatedly, Christian poverty is first and foremost an internal attitude, an internal orientation that finds external expression in different ways. A religious will always try to integrate that internal attitude with the external observance. This will mean that even though he uses creatures in a spirit of moderation and discretion, at the same time he will not be fearful of the risk taken in using creatures. So long as things at his disposal can be used in the spirit of the kingdom and for the kingdom, he will feel free to take the risk of using them. Whether this is the use of money, or buildings, or material things, or services, or talents, or developed skills, or time — as long as they can be used for the greater glory of God, and as long as his specific religious vow does not deny their use — the poor religious will use God's creatures in God's service. In a very real sense, his vow of poverty makes him a free man, free with the freedom of being a child of God.

But still, being human and being as yet in a very human condition, the religious vowed to poverty should not close his eyes to the captivating fascination of possessions. Even the most sensitive man of faith cannot ignore the powerful enticements that God's creatures exert on him. Creatures were made by God to be enticing; no man can expect them to lose their attraction just because he decides not to let creatures control him. Money, property, possessions, education, degrees, travel, books, food, equipment — all these things are enticing. Every man wants to control or to use the whole gamut of created things. He wants to dispose of them as his own. Man has a tendency to remove all things from common use, and wall them in as his own property, and put up the usual sign, "No Trespassing." An increase in possessions in this way, he feels, means a corresponding increase in the value and dignity of his person. Man's possessions, for instance, seem to increase the ambit of his personality.[12] This is the common experience of every person, no matter what creed or code he follows.

Christ, who is God, chose to become incarnate among us and chose to be poor. That fact, and that fact alone, is the only basis for religious poverty that makes any sense — theologically, philosophically, or existentially. Christ gave us this as a philosophy of life. He broke down all barriers between us by being poor himself — the barriers between the divine and the human. The imitation of Christ — this poor Christ — is recommended by Vatican II so very highly in its decrees as well as in its spirit that it is difficult to miss the point. Following this example, religious should be able to live in community with that intensity of love which should bind "the poor" together. It is this intensity of living together in a loving community that will be witness — both for the individual and for the community — to all men. Only by this kind of imitation of Christ will the true "see how they love one anther" witness be given all men.

---

12. "Possessions and Poverty," A New Creation, August Brunner, pp. 36-65.

seven

Religious Obedience

Man and Freedom:

If any ideas have been bandied back and forth in discussions during the last few years, certainly none has been exchanged more than freedom. No one will deny that at times, even rather recently, discussion on freedom has been even intense. Nor will anyone who followed closely the proceedings of Vatican II deny that the discussion on religious freedom was "full, free, and vigorous." Little wonder that Paul VI called the *Declaration on Religious Freedom* "one of the major texts of the Council."

The renewal of insight into many of the traditional concepts that form the basis of religious obedience, as well as the new creative insights into the meaning and living out of religious obedience, have to be understood in the entire context of freedom, authority, responsibility, and obligation as they have developed in the world today. Once again, it is necessary to repeat that religious obedience and the vow of obedience are analogous concepts. Not only has the concept of freedom, as well as authority, developed over the years, but as a result, in a very real sense, religious obedience has developed too. Obedience, like freedom, is not a static concept. It is very much a part of the dynamic of religious life.

Freedom? What does it mean to man today in a very fast developing, socially-conscious ethos? Freedom has to be situated. Few people today honestly believe that any man is absolutely free. Some men confuse freedom and license, true. But most people would be willing to admit that no man is an absolute; no mere man is God. Freedom for most men means some kind of spontaneity — his own inward ability to have and to find reasons for doing things and to motivate himself to action apart from any external forces and pressures. To be oneself, to be genuine, to be honest in pursuing truth and to grasp the truth tenaciously — these constitute the inner core of freedom as man sees it today.

Man experiences freedom not as an absolute nor a complete opening to a life of license. In fact, just the opposite. The existential response to freedom is responsible action. It can almost be said absolutely that man experiences freedom as a duty to be or to do something. For example, man has a fundamental option, as we saw in chapter one, to be a man. His response to this option is the acceptance — a free choice of course — of the duties of being a man. The same is equally true of all three options open to man. Freedom, then, opens out to man on the three option levels: fundamental option, love option, and state of life option. Corresponding to each of these freedom options are responsibilities connected with each. To each free response are attached claims of justice, law and also the guidance of legitimate authority. If I choose, for instance, to be a man, others can claim the right to be treated like men. If I choose to be a loving Christian, others can claim my love. If I choose to be married, others can claim their rights in marriage. We can see immediately why it can be said that the highest and most significant meaning of freedom is in love, because in love most is given and most is demanded.

Man As Person:

The one most important development that has contributed more than anything to our modern concept of freedom is the consciousness we have of the meaning of person. No single metaphysical, psychological, or social concept has captivated man's recent thinking as much as the meaning of being a person. Much of our thinking over the centuries was controlled and dominated by nature-centered thought: the meaning of man's nature, natural law, human nature in Christ, etc. As we shall see later, this excessive concentration on nature resulted in a heavily concentrated emphasis on law and the obligation of law.

Tremendous growth has taken place here. Not that there had been in the past an oversight in this important area, but rather, man had to grow into this consciousness of himself as a person, of how to act as a person, and of the relationship between himself as person and a community of persons. This insight into himself as a person has helped him realize responsibilities not only of himself as having a human nature but of himself as a person. And this, more than anything, has made a significant change in his thinking and in his responses.

For life as a person opens up to man vistas that he could not appreciate otherwise. At the same time, life as a person has broadened his responsibilities. For now man as a person realizes that he must not only conform to nature's patterns and laws, but that he himself is to a great extent himself responsible for these very patterns and laws. For the first time, seemingly, man suddenly has become aware of something he has known for a long time conceptually but now realizes existentially. Man realizes he is not merely an individualized human being. He realizes, now, that his selfhood finds fulfillment only in being a person in community and in his response to "the other."

What a difference that makes! To realize selfhood fully, man now realizes he must be creative — he creates himself as a person. Suddenly man seems to have realized that he cannot live centered around and in himself but must interact with others. By thus interacting with others in "I-Thou" encounters, he is asserting himself, creating himself as a person. God gives him this power.

Freedom and responsibility have to be seen in the light of this kind of personalism today. So, too, must man's response as created responsibility to law and to authority be seen in the light of a personalistic line of thought. In the past, frequently, authority and the human response to authority, namely obedience, were situated almost exclusively under the heading of law. Similarly, human responsibility was looked upon almost exclusively as the normal, healthy response to authority and to law. This has created a problem — many problems in some instances. How be spontaneous? How be free? How have initiative? How even be a person if law and responsible action under law hampers all these? Man living under law seems to lose the very thing that made growth possible: creativity. The very things seemingly needed for the fullness of personhood — initiative and creativity — seemed to be removed in the life dominated by law.

Man is not liberated from limiting institutions and constructs of the past instantaneously. Growth into the full freedom of a person is a gradual thing. This is what makes the entry of every Christian into a full life of freedom a rather difficult thing. This is what is making the full meaning of being free, being a person, making one's own options in life, living under a personalized, authority/obedience structure in the Church today such an anguished development.

Christ, the Christian and Obedience:

For the Christian who responds to the love option, authority and obedience to authority have meaning only insofar as they bear a relationship to Christ. The Christian encounters "the other," and in "the other" also encounters Christ. Freely the Christian accepts this encounter as a loving response, and at the same time freely accepts the responsibility of that love. Here is the link for every Christian with Christ. Christ, too, responded in a human love-encounter: To be fully human and in love with man and his human condition. He accepted this condition and all that it meant, as Vatican II so clearly states, "on mission from his Father."[1] His love response, as Vatican II again tells us, to the human condition was "to carry out the will of the Father. . . . By his obedience he brought about redemption." In other words, love of the human condition, love of man, was shown by doing the will of his Father. Not a vague, nebulous, undetermined will of the Father by any means! For Christ the will of the Father was expressed in his birth at Bethlehem; his very human life at Nazareth; his friendships with the Apostles, disciples, and women friends; his public life; his passion, death and resurrection — these were the existential realities that spelled out his Father's will. To this his Father's will, Christ was obedient to his death on the cross.

The Christian, too, responds in obedience to the Father's will through and with Christ. As with Christ, the Christian responds to the Father's will which concretely means the circumstances established by Christ in his Church. The Christian freely enters into a loving relationship with the Christian community, the Church. And this for him is a liberation. With the early Christians, entry into the Church was like a liberation from slavery; for the Christian today it is the liberation from the slavery of sin and selfishness. The Christian should see his commitment to the Christian community as a passage from self-centeredness, anxiety, and fear into a life of joy, love and service.

Yet, the very heart, the inner core of that Christian community is authority. The loving response to that authority in the Christian community is obedience. It demands, really, the same kind of obedience as Christ's obedience since both are instances of a response to the will of the Father. Thus, we can truly say that every Christian is called to obedience and that the obedience to which he is called is obedience to the authority of the Church.

---

1. Vatican II, C.C. #3.

All too often in the past, the personal element of this response has been overlooked. The Church has been looked upon purely and simply as a legal organization with rules and laws to be obeyed. As a result, obedience as a personal response to a personal authority has been often overlooked. Authority in the Church has all too frequently looked upon itself as a court of law — decrees, law, commands, and rubrics, were its most favored expressions. These soon became absolutes! As with the Scriptures so with authority-figures in the Church, a certain amount of demythologizing has to take place. This can be done, and as a matter of fact is being done, by the process of personalization and a revivification of the spirit of service so well epitomized by Christ as the "servant of all servants." When all is said and done, this much becomes evident: Every Christian with the help of God's grace must ultimately, under freely chosen authority, attain freedom for himself. Harboring resentment toward authority achieves nothing for Christians but a return to slavery. Dominating Christians by legalistic formulations achieves nothing for authorities in the Church except fearful and resentful childish rebellion. Only the realization of personal freedom on the part of authorities and on the part of committed Christians can bring about a joyfully integrated loving community.

Religious Vow of Obedience:

How is all this related to the religious vow of obedience? It is impossible to understand the development that has taken place, rather recently, in the theology of evangelical obedience apart from what has been said above. The development has been to a very great extent personalistic. Not that the basic ideas have not been there for a long time, or that all of a sudden, modern man has made a completely new discovery: Biblical obedience. Rather, historical circumstances have forced religious to re-examine and review some rather basic and traditional authority structures.

The traditional concepts of authority and obedience in religious life were basically sound and served excellently well in the historical milieu in which they were lived out. The best proof for this is the many examples of glowing heroism and sanctity witnessed throughout the history of religious life. No one can honestly argue that religious men and women responded so generously in spite of "the system." Nor do the facts prove that most of them sanctified themselves because of the obstacles encountered in religious life. Even after hagiography has been demythologized, the bare historical facts prove over and again the soundness and efficacy of traditional concepts when properly applied.

Nonetheless, no one will deny that these same traditional concepts, when overemphasized or absolutized in practice, produced not saints to be canonized but caricatures of sanctity. For example, an apt and very meaningful analogy of a religious practising "blind" obedience degenerated into the image of an obedient religious as lifeless and utterly submissive, as a person who has surrendered his most precious human right so that he could be free from further personal decision-making. All too often religious obedience became identified with passivity. A very strange dilemma resulted in religious life: An either/or choice between initiative or obedience. Seemingly, a religious had to choose between accepting passivity or rejecting obedience. Such a dilemma could hardly result in choices which would lead to happiness, and much less to heroism.

A New Art:

In a now rather famous (among Jesuits) talk on obedience given to the members of the Thirty-first General Congregation of the Society of Jesus, Very Reverend Pedro

Arrupe, the Superior General of the Jesuits, emphatically stressed the fact that in religious life today "there is a certain new *art* of governing and an *art* of obeying that must be learned."[2] There has to be a new "art" of both governing and obeying because of the developments that have taken place. I would like to point up four such elements, all of which are mentioned in one way or another in the talk by Father Arrupe.

Obedience and God's Will:

First of all is the thorny problem of just how a superior's will manifests the divine will to us. It is very hard to believe that over the course of centuries all the examples of domineering superiors have been the result of psychological power-drive problems of superiors. The instances in which popes, bishops, pastors, religious superiors — both men and women — and other superiors have succeeded in presenting an image of authority or sheer power have been too frequent to brush them off as merely psychological problems. This projection of a power-image may have been traced in some instances, to such a psychological root cause. But it seems more realistic to say that the very structure of both ecclesiastical and religious authority fostered a kind of power-image. The superior, the one in authority, was almost always looked upon as one apart, a leader set apart and often above the crowd, the people, the community. Even the symbols of authority emphasized this same "one-set-apart" theme: Special clothing, special title, special seating, special greeting. A superior was a personality set apart. Then, too, theologically the usual impression was that through a grace of office and a special call from God, superiors had greater

---

2. Cf. "A Talk on Obedience," Pedro Arrupe, S.J. **Woodstock Letters,** Fall, 1967 pp. 428-434.

surety that their decisions — because they were superiors appointed by God — were the better, or even the best in a particular human situation because of this divine election. This kind of power-image and the corresponding symbols attached to this image gradually reflected backwards in such a way that subjects were made to believe that superiors were more gifted by God — intelligence, morals, vision, etc.— than those over whom they have been placed. What could develop, and what did develop in some dioceses, parishes and religious communities, was a caricature, a distortion of authority and obedience.

Obviously, authority and its counterpart, obedience, are essential to the Church of Christ, and therefore to religious communities. An ideal of a collectivity with no need for authority or obedience is purely and simply "pie in the sky." On the other hand, the new art of governing has to see authority as a proper balance between superior and community. A superior must manifest authority, it is true, but not as a father leading his little children. A superior, today, in community must be a brother among brothers (or a sister among sisters). As a brother among brothers, a superior may well show his lesser intelligence, his deficiencies, his human limitations, and even his moral defects without fear. But in spite of all this, he is no less a superior who represents the authority of God. In fact, it may well be that because of the realization of these very deficiencies and limitations, the superior humbly acknowledges that ways have to be constantly found by which he, as superior, along with all the community seek the will of the Father.

Understandably, the insight of the past has been used as the basis of further insight. It is very true that the Holy Spirit works in and through superiors. But that is not all. He is working also in each individual within the community. He is working in the milieu, the events, the happenings of the time too. Only when all these factors are brought together — the superior working with the community, events, milieu, etc. — can the divine will be found. All these things have to be carefully and prayerfully considered. I say "prayerfully" because one of the tasks of the superior is, ultimately, to discern what is best to be done as the divine will. The divine will should not be considered a blueprint waiting to be discovered in prayer.

The Spirit works in all members of the community, in one way or another, but the superior has to make a final decision as to what manifestation of the Spirit is the true will of God. Many in the community may work together in the process of decision making, but the final decision rests with the superior. The response to this final decision of the superior is religious obedience.

With or without rules for discernment — for the Spirit breathes where he will — a superior today must make use of the dynamic and spiritual cooperation of the community entrusted to him. Humbly admitting his own strong and weak qualities, intelligently ferreting out information from those more qualified than himself, maturely refusing to treat his brothers in Christ as immature little children — a superior today has to carry on his task of directing his community in a new way. The superior has to consider himself a servant to the community with whose help he makes the decision as to what God's will is. It should be obvious that a new art of governing is painstakingly developing.[3]

---

3. No single essay has been more instrumental in reshaping the basic structure of religious obedience, (I can certainly speak at least about Jesuits and of all those whom they influence) than Father Karl Rahner's "A Basic Ignatian Concept: Notes On Obedience." (Reprinted in **Christian in the Market Place**, pp. 157-181.) Since this essay was first published before Vatican II — in German in 1955 — it may well be that Father Rahner would want to change or to modify some of his ideas or the expressions used. However, the basic thrust of this pre-Vatican II essay is still the basic thrust in post-Vatican II days.

The Art of Dialogue:

Secondly, we can talk all we want to — until the Second Coming, if we have the time — about the very basic ideas that no superior should act as if he is God himself. Or about the fact no merely human laws should be too readily absolutized. Or that decision-making is neither the prerogative of an aristocracy in the community nor the compellent compendium of a collectivity. Unless some new means and new methods are used today by which members of a community can present their ideas to the superior, little adaptation or progress will take place. Unless members of a community through some form of personal representation make their attitudes, ideas and feelings known to their superior, apostolic dynamism degenerates into pure passivity.

It is not sufficient today for any religious superior to shrug off responsibility by saying, "My door is always open; let them come in." Who knows but that some timid religious may consider that image as an open door to a lion's den and not want to disturb the inmate. Certainly, personal representation of one's difficulties, objections, problems, and ideas through personal conversation is always helpful. But more than this is required in community today. Some kind of structured dialogue has to be inserted into community whether that be dialogue through councils, group dynamics, brainstorming sessions, committees, group meetings, or common community conferences. Through dialogue of this kind a healthy confrontation takes place between the discussion of the group and the personal character of the superior who must make decisions. Dialogue on a much larger scale than person-to-person conferences is called for and even demanded today. In fact, it is an absolute necessity that institutional means for achieving active dialogue be introduced into community life.[4]

Thus, through dialogue within the entire community, the image of complete passivity, so often suggested by some of the more classic formulae, will be avoided. Having dialogue before decision is made implies the active cooperation of the whole organization. Dialogue in a religious community calls for real honesty in communication as well as a trust in the fact that the other person has honestly thought out and presented his ideas. It is hardly possible to be a passive member of a community if one's heart and mind are involved in communication; if one tries to make himself loveable and loving in dialogue; if one strives to find through dialogue a union of heart and mind with other members of the community. Dialogue in a community should become the active, common seeking of God's will. In rhythmic movement, through communication in dialogue, information is gathered; a decision follows through the final judgment of the superior, and this decision calls for obedience on the part of the members of the community.

Just as the vow of obedience cannot mean merely a passive commitment to rules and commands of superiors, neither can it mean a surrender of personal responsibility. And yet, some traditional images and analogies used to express obedience seemed to lend themselves to the misinterpretation of handing over to a superior one's own personal responsibility. For instance, we are familiar with the comparison of an obedient person being "like a staff in the old man's hand." Or the very venerable expression of a perfect religious practicing "blind obedience"— as if it meant that one deliberately had to shut his eyes to the implications

---

4. An excellent summary of the meaning of dialogue and an application of dialogue — even though in another context — will be found in Pope Paul's first encyclical, **Ecclesiam Suam,** part 3.

of his act and even the consequences for the future. This, then, is the third element in the changing concept of the art of obeying that needs explanation.

Dialogue is necessary in community today — this we have seen. Decision by the superior must follow, lest dialogue continue into meaningless and endless debate. What is the response of an active member of the community to the decisions that follow dialogue? It should be responsible obedience, or in other words, an eager and prompt acceptance. Obedience of this kind which follows representation and dialogue, when dialogue is necessary, is not merely an unquestioning or irresponsible submission. Superiors and members interact in a community in an authority-obedience process. A cooperative interaction results. Notice, the result is not collective government. The result is, rather, an interaction in dialogue that concerns itself with the common good and ends in a decision made by the superior. Both the superior and the members are active.

"Blind Obedience":

But, then, what of "blind obedience" and the supernatural dimension of religious obedience? Why is faith necessary if only a response to dialogue is called for? To answer these questions, a few clarifications are needed. It should be much clearer now that "blind obedience" should not be unquestioning submission. On the other hand, once a process of representation through communication has taken place, once proper recourse has been made, then a responsible submission may well be called "blind obedience." If a decision has been made for the community good, members should turn their own attentions from the reasons "against" to the reasons "for" an action. This is not an anti-intellectualism by any means because every mature person will strive to find as many positive reasons as possible to follow the decision.[5] If dialogue has been healthy, then many of these reasons should not be too difficult to find as they were already discussed in dialogue. Perhaps in the past, too much emphasis was placed on the act of the will. Even before one had dialogue, if one wanted to be more perfect, he obeyed with "blind obedience." It was almost as if "blind obedience" initiated the process and was merely a will-act that easily accepted all that was commanded. Now we see more clearly that perfect obedience is the response of the whole person even to the deepest and innermost depths of love. So now we can see a "blind obedience"— if we must use that phrase — as the cheerful acquiescence at the *end* of a process. So much so that if enthusiasm is very evident at the end of the process, especially if the decision is contrary to what one had dialogued for, this is a sure sign of great love.

However, it is impossible to have dialogue all the time either in person with the superior alone, or with the entire community. There just is not that much time in one's day. Besides, many things happen in community and many decisions are made that ordinarily should require no dialogue. Many of the small rules and regulations, the order of the day, observances of silence and quiet — even though they may have ascetical value — should be looked upon, more and more, as means to coordinate the common good of the community. Every human being, no matter who, is called upon to abide by rules and regulations which help to make life run more smoothly for all. Every Christian is called upon to accept set methods of responding to others in a spirit

---

5. Every religious community should have some standard method of procedure for handling cases of conscience within the community. The procedure should allow for those cases in which a religious feels a true conflict between conscience and the decisions of superiors. If time and again a religious runs into this kind of conflict, serious consideration should be given to regard some other way of serving Christ rather than in religious life. (This was the serious conclusion of the Jesuits at their Thirty-first General Congregation in regard to matters of conscience.)

of love. Every religious, also, is called upon to accept in daily life many small details that make life in community more happy. Negative responses to authority in instances of this kind should be interpreted more frequently as indications of immaturity rather than as signs of religious disobedience. On the other hand, positive responses to an authority which expresses itself even in small things, can and frequently do indicate in the person obeying a living faith and an ardent charity. Like faith, obedience is a positive and a certain virtue, but it is nonetheless obscure — sometimes even hidden in minute details and rules. Like charity, obedience tries to see the person behind the law, but that too can often be obscure. Religious obedience always has to be situated in faith and charity, and at the same time, only in faith and charity can it be truly found.

Art of Delegation:

The fourth and final dimension that has to be considered because of a new opening out to development is what we might call delegation of authority. Once again it is necessary to insist that the matter of delegation of authority should not be treated as a novel supplement to traditional obedience but rather as a traditional concept looked at from a new aspect. In the traditional notion of obedience and authority, it seems that the most frequent attitude always started at the top with authority and filtered down to obedient subjects. A very high premium was put on conformity and on carrying out the command of the superior to the very last and least details. Within the monastic structure of religious life this notion of obedience was quite operative and practical. But as religious life developed into more and more apostolic forms, even though conformity was necessary, some new and improved techniques were needed. If the apostolic works were to be successful and operable, and if some degree of efficiency were to be expected, more initiative and creativity had to come from the bottom. Little wonder that the principle known as "subsidiarity" began to be applied to religious life too. In a sense, the basis of "subsidiarity" in religious life is the trust and love the superior has for persons in the community. So much so that he entrusts others with doing jobs, initiating projects, making arrangements and working out details as if that other member of the community were his other self. This, too, is a form of communication: The superior communicates himself to others and then trusts in their responses. Initiative, creativity, experimentation, change — all these are responses from "down below" that a superior today, in a spirit of trust and charity, must expect and be ready to accept patiently. Even more, the superior today must be willing, besides allowing members of the community to be creative and to have initiative, also to permit mistakes, faults, and even costly errors. Certainly, prudence is necessary, but prudence should not be identified with inaction. In religious life, delegation means trusting the other as though he were another self. Every superior knows that "his own self" has faults, makes mistakes, is weak. Why should he be surprised or full of fear when he discovers the same limitations in other members of the community?

Subsidiarity in religious life has to be seen against the background of service. All religious, superiors and members alike, have committed themselves to service — sometimes something very special and unique — to their community, to the Church, to all men. Through service, of whatever kind it be, they strive to give glory to God, and at times, even greater glory to God. It is always for the very purpose of ordering this service to others and for others that superiors are needed within the religious community as well as in any Christian community. Both superiors and members within the community have to be guided by the same spirit of service. Confronted with the demands of better and greater service, superiors cannot be satisfied with the mere issuance of commands and directives. This is just one aspect of delegation and subsidiarity. Superiors must not only speak; they have to listen too! Superiors have to recall constantly that those to whom they delegate matters are also urged on by and committed to service of their fellow man. Superiors have to realize that others, too, are active, responsible, creative, and are willing and very able to direct and dominate all their own direction of others by love. Superiors must not only listen but take to heart what they hear, for the Holy Spirit, more often than we realize, speaks through others. This is how a superior, today in our present age, exercises service to the community. His *diakonia* is a new art but retains still the overtones of the Christ-example of washing the feet of the apostles.

Functions of Authority:

Obedience, therefore, cannot be fully understood apart from authority and the role of authority. To understand the meaning and implication of obedience as a loving response of a member of a community, the role of a superior within that community has to be fully understood. We mentioned that a superior's role is a *diakonia*, a service to the community on the level of interpersonal love. Just how should this service manifest itself in the superior of a religious community? In a talk, and later in an essay on "Freedom, Authority, Community,"[6] Father John Courtney Murray, S.J., speaks of the three basic functions of authority in the Church and the three corresponding functions of the Christian. These same functions serve as a most apt basis of structure for authority

---

6. The talk was given at Woodstock, Maryland at the "Search and Service Institute," August 7-12, 1966. I am also indebted to other members of the Institute for some ideas which I heard for the first time at Woodstock and have tried to express in this book. Father Murray's article was later published in **America**, December 3, 1966.

and obedience in religious life. Using Father Murray's frame-work, we will discuss first of all the three functions of a religious superior in community and then the three functions of members of a community. All these functions, both of superiors and members, have to be seen as service to the community on the level of interpersonal love.

The first function of a religious superior is the most obvious one of creating a unity, a communion of love. In a very valid comparison, the superior can be said to do what God himself does — he unifies, establishes a harmony of mind and heart, and strives to get a response of heart and mind from all the members. Above, it was pointed out that this kind of unity today can be brought about only by com-munication in the form of one kind of dialogue or other. Also, we have seen, that the highest point of dialogue within the community is in the Eucharistic celebration where Christ, our true superior, communicates himself in loving commu-nion. The superior gathers all things together and draws everyone into a closer communion with each other. The climax of communion is in the community Eucharistic celebration.

But the closeness and intimacy of the Eucharistic com-munion is not possible every moment of the day, even though this kind of loving togetherness and unity is the ideal for which community strives and the promise of things to be hoped for. When "the celebration is over; go in peace" of the liturgy has been pronounced at the end of Mass, the community has been given a mission to perform. Herein rests the second function of the superior: To direct the loving community in its mission, the liturgy of action. This directive function of a superior situates itself most evidently in the decisions that have to be made for the good of the community. Yet, it also must be evident in the superior's direction of members on an individual basis. In all decisions, a superior has to be guided not only by the conclusions of the communication that has taken place but also by the spirit of the institute of a particular religious community, by its laws and rules, and by the demands of the apostolate to which the community is committed. Both singly and collectively, members of a community have to be directed by authority, and more specifically by a listening and loving superior who is attuned to the common good of the community to whose service he is committed.

There is a third function of a religious superior which seems to be somewhat balked at by both superiors and members today. This function has to do with the correction of members. Even granted sincere and honest dedication, even granted that commitment is mature, open, and very willing on the part of all members in a community; yet, in our human condition, there are still faults and shortcomings that need not only correction but even at times concrete reparation to restore right order. As humans, all of us balk at correcting others. And yet, all of us realize how easily we are overcome by our own selfishness and egoism. If the superior's prime function is unifying the community, then it is also his function to correct with condign means and even penalties whatever is a hindrance to communion. Once again, it should be obvious that the ideal is hoped for in community that no such hindrances to unity appear. But neither superiors nor members should be that naive to think the ideal of a loving community is easily or even frequently arrived at without pain, tension, suffering, and positive harm done by even sincere and committed members.

Functions of Members:

Corresponding to the three functions of the superior, are the three functions in community of its members. Just as the superior has a unitive function, so the members respond to the Spirit working in them to help all toward communion. The gift here is charismatic. So much so that it can be said that the first function of the members of a community is a response to the Spirit to aid the superior in creating a loving community. This is creativity at its highest point: A member of the community not only realizes self-fulfillment, but now fulfillment is other-directed in forming a loving-community. Communication here need not be always verbal. Dialogue can take the form of common action, work, participation in a common project, or whatever is considered helpful to creating community. Community is not a place or a given — it has to be created. To help create, with a superior, a communion is the primary task of the members.

Secondly, and corresponding to the superior's second function, is the response function of the members. If the superior has a duty to direct, so also the member has a duty to respond to this direction by loving action. Freely and willingly a member should do his share of the task by carrying out directives of the superior. A loving member of a community willingly accepts his share of the work, the toil, and the cares of community.

At times, this function is looked upon as the cross of community life. It is! To look upon Christian life, and more so, community life, as freedom from sacrifice and the cross is just not realistic. It is the "pie in the sky" that we laugh at in other human panaceas. Our entire orientation to religious community has to be toward freedom, toward making love possible. But very frequently, the *conditions* for freedom and for love have to be realized before one can be free to love. To make myself free and to help make a community free, sacrifice — and very frequently a very penetrating self-sacrifice — is needed. At times this may seem to be an obstacle to self-achievement, but situated in a context of a loving community, sacrifice with and in community makes possible a self-fulfillment far beyond one's own limited, egocentric self.

Finally, the third function of the members in community is self-corrective. Something in our very make-up rouses us almost instinctively against admitting our wrong-doing and even more so against repairing the harm done. The two concepts of mortification and reparation come into play here. Mortification looks to the control of the egocentric dynamisms, and reparation looks to the acts and attitudes needed to restore order, once harm or evil has been done another. Any tendency of yielding to the self, which is also a refusal to open oneself freely to the Spirit, needs a mortifying control. Once the tendency has been yielded to, since harm has been done the common good — the communion is disrupted — some kind of reparation has to be made. The more a member of a community corrects and repairs his own "sins" in community, the more easily will a superior be able to concentrate on his first and foremost function: creating unity. Equally, the less a superior yields to his own egocentric desires and the less self-correction there has to be on his part, the more his dynamisms can be directed to the positive elements in creating community.

Results of Obedience:

By now it should be evident that religious obedience, when it is prompted by love, demands a conscious blend of both vision and determination. An obedient religious has ever before his eyes a vision of a loving community, a communion not yet of saints, but of loving men or women who have hopes of attaining sanctity. Religious obedience does demand the divinization of our passivities.[7] But at the same time, and equally true, religious obedience demands a responsible initiative and creativity. The right-ordering of oneself and the self-containment demanded by creative and responsible obedience makes a religious a better person, a more effective apostle, and with loving and persevering effort, even something of a saint.

---

7. Cf. Teilhard, **The Divine Milieu**, part 2.

eight

Religious Spirituality

Spiritual Pluralism:

Among the many startling and amazing changes taking place in the Church today, one stands out as particularly noticeable. It is the enlightening realization that there can be and actually is in the Church such a thing as pluralistic spirituality. Whether the felicitous expression, "Unity in essentials; diversity in accidentals" sufficiently summarizes the idea, the attitude behind the development is worthy of study. Certainly, this expression, used even by Pope John XXIII, did make many Catholics stop in their tracks, look around at some rather unfamiliar activity going on, and wonder what was happening to them or to the Church. Simply put, for decades and even for centuries, a certain standardization had been taking place: in liturgy, prayer, education, devotions, and even in art, music, and architecture. The word "catholic" took on the meaning of "universally the same and identical." Unity and sameness became the hall mark of Catholics; uniformity developed into a passion for some. Diversity, or Catholic as meaning "comprehensive or universal," was all but forgotten, ignored, or suppressed.

Religious, too, for ages seemingly had been following the same thought and action patterns. A kind of ossification had been taking place which set a uniform standard and pattern for common life, prayer life, apostolic life, and even social life. It was almost a dictum, even though often expressed as a joke that "what was good for the monk was good for the many." It was almost as if a person who entered religious life were given a set of guidelines or rules for sanctifying oneself entitled: "How to become a champion saint in ten easy lessons." Some may respond that this picture of religious life is nothing but a caricature and was not the usual thing. Yet, it did take place and is still seen in some religious communities even after Vatican II.

Unity in Diversity:

There are, obviously, many elements in Christian and Catholic spirituality that must be the same for all. Unity in these things is by all means absolutely essential. The most obvious unifying elements in the Church are its dogmas as revealed by Christ and explained over the centuries by the living magisterium. Christians responding to these revelations of Christ will also show a certain amount of unity in the means they take to express themselves spiritually. For instance, all Christians see the need for prayer in their lives, for some form of liturgical or communal worship, for an other-directed social dimension to their Christian commitment, for at least an attitude toward accepting suffering and pain in their lives, and other things along these general lines. On seeing the need of most of these elements, if not of all of them, Christians are unified. At the same time, just how each person is to give expression to these elements in his own life will vary immensely. There may well be as much diversity in response as there are people in the world. There is not, certainly, this much diversity, but at least this much diversity is possible. Yet, in all their diversity, each must respond to the totality of the Christian revelation.

Ultimately, both unifying and diversifying elements for Christian spirituality lead eventually to one end — union with God or as it often expressed, life-with-God. The Christian strives in all he does — prayer, apostolic work, leisure, liturgy — to find a satisfying and a fulfilling union and life-with-God. This is the aim, the goal, the finality of all spirituality. All men are called by God to this supernatural union with him. How man responds, and to what degree he commits himself to this union, is what we usually mean by spirituality.

Need for Diversity:

Diversity in spirituality, like unity, is absolutely essential. This statement might well have overtones of a dogmatic dictum or of an absolutism, which most seem to want to avoid. And yet, unless diversity is not only permitted but even ardently fostered in spirituality, the changes which have recently been effected may, sooner than we think, themselves become ossified absolutes and once again allow for no needed changes in the Church. Spirituality — that is, man's response to Christ's revelation — has both a unifying principle as well as a diversifying principle.

There is a theological basis for both unity and diversity as the sum and substance of our Christian spirituality. In the very God who reveals himself to us, there is unity as well as distinction. Then too, in the way in which God reveals himself, there is unity in what is revealed but diversity in the manner in which it is revealed. For centuries, now, we have talked about and prayed over the "one nature and the three persons" in God. Substantially, this remains identically true today. The reality — God, three in one — always the same. But our insight and understanding of the reality changes and develops.

Today, we are much more concerned with how God is present as a person in our midst than we are with the fact of his nature and essence. This shift in our understanding — or desire for understanding — makes it not only possible but also imperative that our understanding of spirituality change too. Being conscious of how God is present in our midst in a great variety of ways, and our faith in the diversified presence will have more meaning to us today than merely knowing or saying or making an act of faith in the fact of the defined three persons of the Trinity.

Let us take just one very concrete example. We believe that the risen Christ, a person, is really present in the Eucharistic bread and wine after the consecration. As firmly as ever we believe in transubstantiation. But now we realize even another presence of Christ: Christ present in the community gathered around the Eucharistic banquet table. Obviously, the risen Christ is one and the same no matter where he is. But his presence is realized in different ways at different times and in different circumstances. Today we realize more than ever before that the community gathered together in Eucharistic celebration is not the same as a community gathered in a dining room for a meal. In the Eucharistic community a transignification has taken place. The community has changed into a new, creative gathering, and Christ is present in their midst in a new, signified presence.

The God-Person, who is present in our midst, is present in diverse modes not because of his own limitation but because of the finiteness and limitation which is the very essence of created reality. In fact, God choose to freely limit himself to our own finite mode of existence. The God who has thus freely chosen to limit himself is both transcendent to created reality — by his very being — and immanent to it, by his own free choice. No merely human reality or existence can fully exhaust the infinity of God. Apart from the hypostatic union, in which the divine Son took on a human element and exhausted its finite potential in Christ, finite reality can only partially and in a limited way reflect the infinite.

Diversity in Religious Life:

This consideration, as involved and as abstract as it may sound, is necessary background for consideration of diversity in spirituality, and also for diversity in the forms of religious life. Unless we understand that finite beings and finite forms can express or reflect only limited facets of God's inner life, we will never understand why there is need for diversity in the Church, in spirituality and in religious life.

Let us take liturgical celebration as an example of the point in question. It is not a sufficient explanation to say we have to have different forms of liturgical celebrations merely to fit the varied and different needs of men. There is even a more basic and a more radical reason for diversity. The reason is found in the way God communicates himself to men. Signs or symbols indicate different aspects of the God-life. In some instances when the need is there, liturgical celebration should be solemn, full of splendor, a rich diapason of all man can gather around an ample altar and in an amply adorned church. God's transcendence is manifested by sign and symbol in this type of liturgy. At other times, liturgical celebration should be in a home, or school, or factory — simple, direct, unadorned. God's immanence is reflected and symbolized better in this type of liturgy. For these very same reasons — the sign and symbol values — even the basic structures of liturgical celebrations should be different for different occasions. To be sure, the kind of liturgical celebration should be determined by one's own spirituality. And spirituality is ultimately determined by one's desires and needs.

Just as different kinds of liturgy express, reflect, and symbolize different facets of the God-life, so also do different forms of religious life. Through the different forms of religious life, God is constantly manifesting himself: the one and the same God manifesting himself in diverse modes through signs and symbols. No one form of religious life can completely exhaust the totality of the witness that can be revealed of the God-life. We might say that the forms of religious life in the Church today reflect a broad spectrum of the Trinitarian life of God. In this way, different facets of the God-life are revealed. Looked at concretely, for example, the monastic life with its stability, its solemn liturgical orientation, and its prayerful aura, reflects and manifests a God who is transcendent and above earthly things. At the other end of the spectrum, secular religious life with its absorption in the secular, work-a-day world, reflects and manifests a God who is not only immanent in creation but has become incarnate in this very human condition. In between these two outside extremes on the spectrum, the great shades of variety of apostolic religious life, which reflect the differences of the extremes, reveal and manifest in varying degrees both the immanence and the transcendence of the God-life.

The expression of spirituality in monastic life should be, therefore, different from that of the apostolic religious life. Historically, the thrust of Benedictine spirituality, for instance, is different from Ignatian spirituality. To try to identify the two or to try to fit both spiritualities into a similar modern mold would lose for the Church the richness of the different aspects of the Trinitarian life. A variety of forms of religious life manifests and reveals the depth and height and breadth of the God-life.

Asceticism and Divergent Practices:

We have said that the basic spirituality of the monastic religious should be different from that of the apostolic religious or the secular religious. Each reflects a different aspect of the Trinitarian life and each gives witness in the world in different ways. We have tried to show that this difference will be seen in the different modes of liturgical participation and in the different modes and methods of life which are followed in the various forms of religious life. Another area of divergence in spirituality should also be studied: the asceticism of religious life.

Can it be said that even the ascetical practice should be different for different kinds of religious life? Before answering this question, perhaps it would be good to answer the deeper questions: What is asceticism? How is ascetical practice determined? How is asceticism related to spirituality?

Throughout the course of salvation history certain expressions and certain words have been consistently used to express man's response against self-centeredness, or against evil and sin in his life. Words like abnegation, ascetical practice, mortification, the cross, penance, self-discipline, sacrifice, and self-denial have always been used. There are so many small nuances of meaning between these words and so many fine distinctions in their meaning that now a real need exists to go back to some more basic ideas in the matter. Whether we call the interior disposition abnegation and the exterior response mortification or vice versa, does not make too much difference. Whether self-denial and sacrifice are objectively diverse is another merely academic question. Rather than concentrate on these mere academic problems, a unifying principle has to be determined.

The basic notion of Christian asceticism can be very simply stated. A Christian is one who commits himself wholeheartedly to love of Christ in and through his fellow men.[1] This is the Christian response to the love option. But his very personal and unique existential experience shows him that his love option is more easily made than acted upon. Commitment in words is much easier than commitment shown by deeds. But deeds are necessary, as love

---

1. Father Bernard Häring's neologism: "Adamitic man," to describe the first response on the love option level is very good. He prefers to label the Christian love option as "Christic personalism." These ideas he develops quite extensively in his article: "A Modern Approach to the Ascetical Life," Worship, December, 1965, pp. 635-648.

manifests itself better in deeds than in mere words. Yet, every person knows how difficult loving deeds can be. So there is the tension: in trying to live out the love of Christ in deeds, one's commitment to Christ in words. The tension, the friction, the rub comes from our constant inertia and laziness, or our continuous, reflective self-centeredness, self-glorification, self-justification, or just plain crass selfishness. Call it the effects of an original fall of man, or call it sin, or call it refusal of interpersonal relationship — whatever one calls it, it is the same reality. Man wants to be self-centered and even selfish when he loves another.

Authentic Christian asceticism is really nothing more profound than the Christian's attempt, with God's help, to overcome this selfish inclination. That same selfish inclination may have become even more gripping on one's personality because of the past experience of repeated yieldings to this inclination, or just plain weakness of personality. The Christian sees this inclination as an obstacle to love: love of neighbor, love of Christ, love of the Father. The Christian also sees another connection. He sees clearly that the cross of Christ was carried as an example to the Christian as well as a redeeming act for him. In the "cross-carrying" of Christ, redemption and example are intimately linked. As a follower of Christ, the Christian realizes that following the example of Christ in his "cross-carrying" there is also a redemptive element in his own life. He redeems himself, so to speak, from his own self-centeredness so that he can love "the other," and through "the other" also love Christ more.

Christian asceticism, then, has a very positive purpose. It is not the means we use to appease an angry, wrathful God; it is not a means merely to gain will power over our emotions and drives; it is not merely a private discipline to make us more effective human beings. Christian asceticism has a Christian thrust. It is the constant effort on the part of the Christian to control or to overcome self-centeredness, and thereby to free himself from himself and go out to his neighbor in love. Asceticism is the means we use as Christians to free ourselves from ourselves and thus to make ourselves open to "the other." Christian asceticism has this very Christian purpose: to make oneself as open to the love of others as Christ was and is open to the love of all of us.

Ascetical Practices:

Ascetical practice for the Christian has to be situated in this kind of context. The Christian has to ask himself constantly: "What is hindering my outgoing, positive thrust? What is hindering my love for 'the other,' and therefore, my love of Christ?" It may be money, sex, ambition, jealousy, comfort — whatever man has learned from his personal experience that can hinder this human relationship. Ascetical practice has to be directed toward control of, or ridding oneself of, or overcoming the obstacle that prevents love. Clearly, then, ascetical practice has to be geared to the unique needs of the individual Christian.

Experience shows us that certain practices do help us to control or to overcome some of our selfishness. Yet, because one's problems and obstacles are so unique, every person has to tailor his ascetical practices almost uniquely to himself. For instance, bodily chastisements may have the very opposite effects on two different persons. For one, bodily penances may be well suited to personal asceticism; to another, such penances may create even greater obstacles to love.

The religious must be as committed to asceticism, as should every Christian. The purpose and the goal of ascetical practice for the religious is exactly the same as that of every Christian. It may well be that a religious will have to be more conscious of ascetical practices in his life because of more obstacles within himself to fulfilling his state of life commitment. But the basis of asceticism for the religious is exactly the same as that of every Christian: to overcome one's selfish or self-centered inclinations, and thus to open oneself more to "the other" and to Christ.

Religious and Ascetical Practice:

As has been already shown, different forms of religious life give witness to different aspects of the mystery of the Trinity. At the same time, religious open themselves to "the other" in different ways. Monastic life is quite different in its "openness" from apostolic religious or secular religious. Now let us see if we can answer the question about different ascetical practices in different forms of religious life.

To be open constantly to "the other," and, for the religious, to be able to give witness to different facets of the Trinitarian life, there is need of a constant integration within one's life. To live-with-God constantly, one has to realize for himself, existentially, both the transcendence and the immanence of God with whom he lives. Recall what was said earlier in the chapter that God cannot communicate the totality of his Trinitarian life to any mere creature — apart from the hypostatic union in Christ. At the same time, every Christian is called upon to imitate Christ — to integrate and to realize within himself both the transcendence and the immanence of the God-life. In monastic religious life, which manifests more fully the transcendent features of the God-life, great emphasis is put on liturgical celebration, prayer, *lectio divina,* recollection, and study. The temptation or the tendency in this form of life is to live an angelic life, a life apart, a life of a disembodied spirit: all soul and no body. Or at least there is a drawing away from the material into a life of an embodied spirit. But the monastic religious is, nonetheless, still very human, still very much a part of the human condition. To realize this even more acutely, asceticism for the monastic religious has taken the form of bodily austerity: fastings, watchings, corporal chastisements, manual work, and other employments. Such forms of ascetical practices are apropos to this form of life. Such ascetical practices help the monastic religious realize that they, too, have an apostolate among men, not only of soul-saving but of body-saving too. Through ascetical practices of this type, monastic religious unite themselves with man in his human condition with all its physical, bodily sufferings and pains. Thus, through the realization of the limitations and weakness of their bodies, they come to an existential experience of the human condition: suffering man, carrying his cross of physical, bodily weakness.

Ascetical practices should be quite different for the apostolic religious. Most apostolic religious are already bound by a strict work schedule: teaching, hospital work, administration, counseling, and a thousand other apostolic employments. They do not have to look outside their very apostolate for ascetical practices that make them conscious of the body as part of our human condition. For them, asceticism will have to take another form. Their basic self-centeredness concerns activity, contact with others on a verbal level, and constant outgoing action in which they are always tempted to seek their own glory and greatness rather than God's greater glory. For apostolic religious ascetical practice will not only be found in the work to be done, the needs and demands of one's profession, the schedule of one's activity, the constant rubbing of elbows with others, but on the other hand, in seeking the transcendent God in private prayer, and silent converse with God, in a quiet recollection, coupled with meaningful conversation with others as required by the needs of the moment. As a human person dedicated to Christ, an apostolic religious, more than any other Christian, has also to be conscious of the needs of others regarding prayer, study, work, rest, and an atmosphere of prayer. He has to learn to respect these rights and needs.

The asceticism and ascetical practice for secular religious will be different too. Living in the heart of the secular world,

and living a life very much like the layman, the member of
the secular institute must find in study and work, in leisure
and recreation, ascetical practices that will help control the
sources and the roots of self-centeredness. Merely to ape the
ascetical practices of monastic religious or apostolic religious
will never, completely and adequately, serve the purpose.
Sometimes the ascetical practice for secular religious may be
nothing more glamorous than developing patience and
allowing God to work in the milieu with the rhythm of
organic growth. Patience — is a difficult ascetical practice in
a push-button, instant-mix world of people; in a world that
loves high speed and fast drive and laughs at slow-moving
man and nature.

Theories of Asceticism:

The biblical asceticism to which every Christian has
committed himself is truly based on a very simple principle.
The Scriptures tell us to deny or control our self-centered
reactions, to act in this way because Christ himself showed
us the way — our action is like his "cross-carrying"— and to
keep going out to "the other" because that is following
Christ.[2] Yet in spite of all its simplicity, various theories
have been proposed as valid explanations of biblical asceticism. For instance, some propose the "Sentimental Theory":
Choose to do only those things which Christ did and use
only the creatures Christ used. Even a secluded monk in
the desert today could not follow this to the letter. Or then,
some propose what I call the "Numbers Theory": Use as
few creatures as you possibly can; the more holy a person is,
the fewer creatures he has to use. This is a rather simplistic
solution for a twentieth century Christian, whether he be a
layman, a monastic or an apostolic religious. Sometimes this

---

2. For an excellent discussion of: "Self-denial according to the Gospels,"
see W. K. Grossouw, **Spirituality of the New Testament**, Chapter 5.

theory is linked with a Manichaean myopia — all creatures that cause pleasure should be eliminated from one's life. Christian asceticism is not and cannot be built around the principle that matter is evil or that creatures are evil. Another theory states that Christian asceticism is built around the idea that the "more difficult" is the more Christ-like, and therefore, the "more difficult" should always be chosen as a more perfect thing. This theory lends itself to a very static notion of asceticism; for instance, some very painful bodily chastisements, such as wearing a hairshirt, because it is more difficult should then be the better ascetical practice and the most Christ-like. The fallacy is only too evident.

Christian asceticism of today, which has grown out of and developed from biblical asceticism, must put greatest emphasis on the following of Christ — not slavish imitation or super-ego compulsive drives — and the denying or the control of selfishness which hinders the following of Christ. Very frequently, the grist for ascetical practice is found in the very passivities of one's life: the things that man has to undergo as a result of being a human being, a Christian, and a religious or married person.[3] All these, the Christian must learn to bear just as Christ has shown him how. But the "cross-carrying" has to liberate him, free him from himself, and open him to the love of his fellow man. If it doesn't do this, then stoic self-sufficiency results.

For a religious, some of these passivities are intimately connected with the form of religious life that has been chosen; they flow from the very nature of the life. These passivities, accepted in the spirit of Christ, help to sustain him and to aid him in growth. But at times, grist for ascetical practice has to be found elsewhere. But just as for any Christian, so for the religious, the ascetical practices decided upon must have an existential dimension to them that links

3. It would be good to read once again Teilhard's "The Divinisation of our Passivities," The Divine Milieu, Part Two.

or integrates them with everyday existence. Ascetical practices should be, as we have seen, very practical. They should, as much as possible, be part of one's daily life and one's life commitment.

Practical Asceticism:

Let us take just one concrete example to exemplify this basic Christian ascetical thrust. Every apostolic and secular religious community is committed to some very specific apostolic works. Religious who are committed to education, for example, should develop and make use of every quality of mind and body God has given them. They ought to commit themselves to a development of knowledge and skills in business, in the teaching profession, in other professional and social skills, and even in artistic appreciation. Such a commitment necessarily demands a very close integration of spiritual formation, the work of study, and along with this, apostolic activity as well. Within this very process of integration is contained the grist of asceticism. This might aptly be called "the asceticism of the academic." The pressures, tensions, cares, discipline, competition, and strains of study are the freely chosen ascetical practices of this commitment. No need to look for other more traditional forms. Penances, bodily chastisements, fastings, vigils may well be valid, traditional forms but more proper, perhaps, to another kind of religious life. For the religious in an academic apostolate, just as for any religious or layman, ascetical practice is excerised primarily, humbly, and simply in the everyday demands of one's commitment.

Religious spirituality, and with it asceticism and ascetical practices, aims always at holiness and perfection. No matter what the form of religious life may be, religious must be motivated by the same enduring desire to live a life-with-God and give witness to the Trinitarian God-life. No matter how diverse the patterns of spirituality may be and are, all are unified and integrated by the religious, the person himself. If the mode of religious life emphasizes too much the spirit, the other world, future life, then religious asceticism will be a deeper involvement in the bodily, the material elements of life. The religious will have to learn by ascetical practice that God is not merely transcendent but immanent, too, in the very material things one has to learn to use; he finds God there too. If, on the other hand, the mode of religious life emphasizes too much the here-and-now, the existential moments of time and space, then religious asceticism may have to discover deeper involvement in some of the more spiritual, and more intensely inner-life elements of existence.

There is no universal blueprint for holiness nor for religious asceticism. Nor is there an ideal image or model religious that can be set up as a goal to be aimed at by all. Sound psychology and good theology tell us that the idealized image, the glamorous, fictitious and fanciful image of the "ideal religious" is nothing more than pure fiction.[4] Guiding one's religious life by such an image; trying to conform to standardized, traditional patterns uniformly imposed as sanctifying molds for all religious — the result will be only frustration, unhappiness, and certainly not the sheer joy that accompanies Christ-conscious rather than self-conscious sanctity.

4. Hugh P. O'Neill, S.J., has given a vivid description of the idealized image of self in his short, acute article, "The Concept of Personal Value," published privately by the University of Detroit Press.

nine

Religious Life - Past, Present, and Future

In the course of our study of changes in religious life, it becomes evident that many elements of the life keep recurring and reappearing, now one way, now another. Many traditional aspects of religious life are basically the same — yesterday, today and forever. For instance, the need for private, daily prayer; concern over recollection that fosters the life-with-God; a relationship between the life in community and the life without; and a basic relatedness of the religious life with "cross-carrying." How do these traditional features, we now ask, relate to our life in the present and in the future?

The Distant Past:

Like every other institution in the Church, religious life has had its ups and downs. Just as the Papacy, for instance, flourished or declined according to the abilities, enthusiasm, holiness, and interest of individual Popes, pretty much the same can be said of religious life. On the one hand, religious life has had its Golden Age, Silver Age, Bronze Age, or Diamond Age — we can almost see them drawn out colorfully on the pages of salvation history. Who of us is not inspired by the sanctity and solitude of Abbot Anthony in the Egyptian desert; we can appreciate why so many good people followed his example. Or who is not impressed by Benedict and his Monte Cassino monks — a new school, at that time, in the Lord's service? Is anyone today unimpressed by the spirit of austere strength and moving love of Bernard of Clairvaux — even though we find his attitudes toward heretics a bit harsh for such a kindly person? Can any man today close his eyes and ears to the message of poverty from the glowing heart of Francis of Assisi? To the love for truth and goodness from the eyes of Dominic? To the zeal and energy and love for Christ in the bold features of Ignatius? Can anyone even today fail to reach out a helping hand to Mother Cabrini's appealing, outstretched hands? The tradition is long and impressive for sure.

Nonetheless, there are some smudged pages in that history, too. We can't just close our ears to what men like G. G. Coulton shout at us.[1] Even in spite of Belloc's counter-thrust,[2] there is still some truth in the charges of historians of Coulton's calibre. It was not always true that monks and friars lived good, exemplary, Christ-centered lives. There are quite a few footnotes in the history of religious life that make for something less than edifying reading. Certainly, it was not the edifying life of religious that from time to time brought about the suppression, and at times demise, of religious institutes.

Something of a balance seems to have been struck over the centuries because, in spite of ups and downs, and maybe even because of them, the dynamism of this life his continued over all these centuries. Right up to our 20th century, this has been true. The tradition of the past — both good and bad — has pushed forward right up into our century. Surprisingly, not only did new types begin to thrive, as for instance, secular institutes, but the older and traditional forms have come along too, sometimes running, sometimes limping, sometimes lagging. But still here!

---

1. **Five Centuries of Religion,** Cambridge, 1923.
2. "The Case of Dr. Coulton," **The Month,** Vol. 170, 1937, pp. 413-419; 493-500.

The Immediate Past:

Spread out and stacked up before me on my desk as I write are many pamphlets, booklets, blurbs, and literature in general on the religious life. Most of the writings reflect the spirit and the thrust of the times in which they were written: pre-Vatican II days. They are the writings that in one way or another appealed to many of us not too many years ago, and helped us make a rather momentous decision in our lives. Their appeal? What was it then? How was religious life pictured then? Usually by a young girl or boy shown with a "halo-vision" overhead; a statue of Christ with arms outstretched; various symbols and signs for thinking out one's vocation; or, are you a religious in disguise? We're familiar with most of them.

This was the time, before Vatican II, that there was a great upsurge in religious vocations, at least in the Western Church; the time that many religious communities, in a grandiose wave of optimism, built and built and built. This was the time when religious were very confident in their methods — they had worked for so many years and centuries, so why not now?

The literature before me reflects very well the spirit of the time. I know, because I was brought up in it. For the time in which they were written, the spirit was good. It was this spirit of religious life, ever so recent, that produced men and women religious who were the dynamic leaders at the time of Vatican II. Weren't Rahner and Congar; Schillebeeckx and Sister Luke; Häring and Sister Marian Dolores; Diekmann and Weigel; Danielou and Durrwell — and countless others, all brought up in this same traditional method? The literature and the systems of religious life reflected by it served the Church quite well, I would say.

What was the spirit, the thrust, the "system" that was able to produce such outstanding religious? It is not too difficult for me to delineate. Perforce, it became a vital part of all of us who were introduced to religious life before Vatican II.

One would almost say that the key idea and the very reason for the success of the pre-Vatican II system was structure: A fixed way of doing things and a very stable way of responding to situations. The structure developed an attitude of mind which usually centered around an elaborate set of rules, regulations, ways of doing things, and so forth. Few of us who went through "the system" will forget, for example, the carefully planned and detailed order of the day in religious houses. Not a minute was to be lost — or even a half-minute.

Somehow, one gets the impression from "the system" of the past, that the idea of having a structure was to be able to come to every life situation fully prepared. Having a plan or a blueprint before approaching a situation assured success. Almost every action of the day was "covered" by a rule or the spirit of the rule. To make a mistake would be almost impossible; mistakes and errors indicated lack of structure.

Nor is it at all difficult to see why so much importance was put on authority from above. With rules and regulations so predominant, it was not at all hard to appeal to the authority in the chain of command. Somehow authority got to mean "something up above"— remote, impersonal, with all the answers.

The literature before me reflects, too, the attitudes and virtues which religious found most important then. Perhaps the most outstanding one was docility. Religious were assured that by being docile to their rules and their superiors, they would surely perfect themselves because this was the divine will. Obviously, an unquestioning, "blind" obedience was called for. Little wonder that the structure took on an attitude of paternalism.

The rigidity of structure served a very good purpose in its day. Those who were in it merely took the structure for granted because they associated it with good common sense. And so it was — then. It served a very definite purpose and achieved many, excellent results. Nor should any of us think that the good religious turned out the way they did in spite of "the system." I don't think that a conclusion of this kind would be fair to them and their sincerity. It would be fairer and more accurate to conclude, I think, that the system then, the structure of yesterday, served the purposes of yester-year very well. The men and women religious who fostered the system and the structure were, for the most part, filled with the wisdom of their times.

Present Day Religious — The Young:

Many of the older religious in communities today were brought up on the pre-Vatican II system. In some instances, this system is still very much operative in communities. However, more and more it becomes evident that a new kind of person is entering religious life today. Also evident is the fact that the former structure of religious life has to be readjusted, not only to fulfill the present needs of the people entering religious life, but also to fulfill the needs of our times.

The young people entering religious life today are not all the same. But there are some very evident similarities: in their attitudes, their desires, their needs, and their visions. These are not always clearly expressed or even understood completely, but they are present, nonetheless.

First of all, it is seen in a kind of healthy and youthful response against "the system" but not necessarily against structure. Young religious today keep asking the question: Is it relevant? Whereas former generations took for granted that "the system" produced what it was meant to produce, not so this generation. Everything is questioned; nothing taken for granted. They do not feel that "the system" and all that it offers is by its very nature either good or bad. The philosophy of "the good old days" does not appeal to them. Therefore, to be handed rules, regulations, procedures, and rites, and to be told "they work," leaves something to be hoped for. Young religious today don't necessarily revolt against structure; they do want to experience its relevancy however.

Experience, in fact, is a key word in their life today. For very many obvious reasons, the young religious does not want to begin with a conclusion — it worked for us before; therefore, it will work for you now. Rather, he wants to experience reality and find out for himself that it is meaningful and relevant. He wants to acquire, perhaps, the same wisdom as his elders, but in a way that is meaningful to him: that is by personal experience. One small example of this, for instance, is a community rule of silence. Not that young religious are against silence, but they have to experience in their own lives the value of quiet and recollection, the value of personal concern for others in the community. No mere words of wisdom from older religious will change this attitude because experience is of prime importance. For the young religious in the world today, this is good, for experience is a preparation to live in today's and tomorrow's world, not yesterday's. This should be a chief concern of every religious.

Secondly, those who respond to the religious vocation today have exactly the same characteristics as their peers in the world today. How describe them? Perhaps the best words to use are: energetic, questioning, generous, open, somewhat idealistic, soul-searching, sometimes naive. For sure, they are not complacent or self-satisfied. Nor do they respond positively to what is rigid or fixed or set. Perhaps the best way to explain this is to say that they are very functional in their approach to reality. They honestly question their own commitments to faith and are openly tense when smug answers are given. Yet, there is an openness and an honesty that no one denies. It is an honesty with themselves and with others that revolts against "phoniness." Something of a fear is evident, too, that they will not be understood or accepted. They want to understand and be understood because they realize that this is the only way they will find Christ in the world today and bring Christ to that world. They see quite clearly the greatness as well as the complexity of the task of life in the world today.

Thirdly, young religious are more concerned than ever about being fully developed persons. Somehow they give the impression that their constant "angst" is to be human, fully human. Not that they reject everything of the past because it was inhuman, but if anything seems to be against what is considered less human or inhuman today, they balk. The expression of this quality is quite revealing. The demands made upon themselves, for instance, are very great. There is such an emphasis on being a person, on being human, that they hardly need to be pushed. They want to work things out on their own and not merely take another's word for it. At times one even gets the impression that there is a kind of "careerism" prevalent among young religious today. Not only do they demand very much of themselves, but from their peers they expect the same generous response. If the response is not forthcoming, they are upset.

But from all appearances this desire to be a fully developed person is not a selfish or self-centered thing. It appears to be more related to others: to help others, to realize their needs, to make rapport more possible. Seemingly, the career attitude links in with their broader social consciousness: their concern for others. For this reason it is not too difficult to help them grow from a highly personal self-realization to a concern for others that is true and rewarding apostolic love. The ingredients for this kind of motivation are certainly present. They have to be brought to the conscious level more and more in the religious community.

Present Day Religious — The Older:

Anxiety best characterizes the older religious in communities today. Ferment, disquiet, great numbers of "lost" vocations, inadequacies, insecurity — the list of evident feelings is long and tedious. And yet, that is not the full picture either. Among very many of them there is a very healthy and wholesome serenity. If anything proves the effectiveness of "the system" of the past, it is the fact that so many religious can remain serene in the face of so much change. In spite of the multitudinous problems facing the world, the Church, and their own communities, there is still prevalent a spirit of composure, a "rolling with the punches." Not a coldness, nor a complacency, but an honest-to-goodness happy realization that the ferment is good.

The most important thing that older religious today can do for the young religious is to prove by a happy and holy life that they are serene in the work of the Lord. Younger religious have to be taught by example how an "I-Thou" encounter can grow and flower out into a "We" relationship. Young religious have to be shown that religious life is not a refuge for the helpless and hopeless, but a truly loving community; not a cloister guarding the insecure, but a community that brings peace to all who enter it. "Peace to all who enter" has to be more than just words written above the front door.

Strange to say, there is already existing a bond that strongly links the old and the young. That bond is the realization that to be human is already to be holy. Both old and young, it appears, link holiness with humanness. For the young, however, humanness will have to include shortcomings, lack of intellectual understanding, ineptitude, failures, lack of brilliance, and even inability to communicate. The young will have to realize that some of these things they see in older members of the community do not make them, thereby, less human or even less holy, for that matter. For the old, humanness will have to include lack of maturity, misguided zeal, idealistic solutions to problems, simplistic approaches to reality, and manifest insecurity. They will have to realize that some of these qualities in young religious do not, thereby, make them less human or even less holy. To be human is to be holy, for sure, but there are degrees of both.[3]

Present Day Religious — Integration:

One wonders, in the light of the good being offered by both young and old in religious life, how the changes that are taking place and are so direly needed can take place more effectively and more smoothly. The answer is not a "two lives" theory — the young and the old living apart as sub-communities. Nor is the answer a rather pessimistic "wait until the old soldiers die" theory. For one thing, even though we speak of the young and old, very frequently the facts do not show such a neat division. Chronological age deceives all too often. Nor is the answer a "wait and see" attitude. If anything, religious should be giving witness to a happy and a holy life. People just don't wait for that kind of witness as something in the future.

No, there is only one solution to the problem, if the problem exists. That solution has already been discussed in the chapter on religious community. Community togetherness in a real spirit of creativity offers the only solution to religious life problems today. No single individual can

3. My discussion of the relationship of the young and old in religious life has been greatly aided by prolonged discussion with other members of a Jesuit Task Force that prepared a position paper entitled "The Jesuit Novitiate — Past, Present, Future." The paper was one of several written for the **Conference on the Total Development of the Jesuit Priest.** Other members of the Task Force were: Fathers Carroll J. Bourg, Andrew J. Brady, and Richard C. Braun. The position paper has been published in **Review for Religious,** Jan. 1968, pp. 121-136.

integrate religious life satisfactorily for an entire community. Nor is a system or structure sufficient. Needed, yes. But sufficient, no! Community as a part of religious life is a continuous, unfolding, process; community is constantly being created. So no matter whether one is a monastic religious or an apostolic religious or a secular religious, there is always need of integration, of synthesis, of community. No structure or system of itself can produce a living, loving community.

A few things should be mentioned here about community as an integration of the contributions of both old and young. Every growing person has a deep concern for his own continuity of self. By "putting on Christ" in religious life no one should be expected to change radically his personality. Nor should one in religious life for any length of time be expected to do this either. In each instance growth can take place only in an atmosphere in which there are opportunities for honest dialogue. In some instances it has been found in religious life that ego identity and social consciousness diminish the longer a person lives the religious life.[4] Actually, this is the exact opposite of what religious life should be and should do for a person.

Now, more than ever before in the long history of religious life, is there need for integration. The young and the old — whether they be that in age or in spirit — have to come to realize that the barriers which divide humanity should not divide religious. What appear as differences and barriers should rather be looked upon as so many gifts and graces from God which he wishes to be integrated. Difficult? Sure! But then so is it difficult to unite spirit and matter. Yet, it has been done.

Probably one of the best ways to integrate a religious spirit is to recall why a particular group of religious was

---

4. See "Ego Identity of the Modern Religious Woman," Mary Howard Dignan, B.V.M., **Journal of Religion and Health,** April, 1967, pp. 106-125.

originally founded. Every particular religious group was founded to do a specific work in the Church and the world. The intention of every founder of a religious group has been that through some form of teamwork and esprit de corps, a group of dedicated religious could perform a specific task in the Church.[5] Obviously, charity is presupposed — both individual and community charity. Two things immediately come to mind: for this to take place there has to be a strong identification with other members of the religious family, and secondly, an identification with the values of that community as expressed by the founder. In spite of the fact that there is so much change going on in the Church and in religious life, through openness, dialogue, and a collective sense of identity with the original thrust of the founder, every religious community today can bear the marks of the Church within itself by being one, holy, catholic, and apostolic. These are the marks of a mature community which identifies itself with something above and beyond itself.

Deterrents of Present Growth:

In the normal course of the development of the human person certain deterrents or obstacles have to be faced and met with at the different levels of growth. All psychologists agree on this, though they don't all agree on what the specific obstacles are or exactly at what stage they are met. In the normal course of development in religious life similar obstacles are met. With different religious, being unique individuals as all humans are, deterrents are met at different times. Often, the obstacles and deterrents to growth differ in time and kind with different religious communities.[6] It

5. For further insight into this aspect of religious life see: "Why Religious Life?" Jean Galot, S.J., **Review for Religious**, July, 1965, pp. 505-517.

6. **Nature, Grace, and Religious Development**, Barry McLaughlin, Newman, 1964.

is not my intention here to outline all the deterrents that religious meet along their road of development nor to specify how they differ in religious communities. I wish merely to point out what I consider major deterrents to present changes that affect all religious, whether they be monastic, apostolic, or secular religious.

First of all, there is the most common problem of individuality. This is a problem of both old and young in religious life. It expresses itself in an "I'm right and you're wrong" attitude. Or again, in an "all black or white" mode of thinking. When expressed in an "either-or" proposition, there is no room for compromise. The result is the development of a self-righteous attitude. Young religious will then have a very critical attitude toward older religious, but not have any healthy, critical attitude toward themselves. And vice versa for older religious — they are critical of the changes, of the new, and of the young, but do not realize that they too should be open to criticism of themselves. In truth, religious life should be big enough to contain both. But this will never be possible unless in practice creative and imaginative coordination of all individuals takes place. No lasting effects of such coordination will ever occur unless among all religious there takes place the realization that compromise is a good, rational, Christian, and religious response. The young must realize that true compromise is not the same as conformity. The old must realize that true compromise does not mean surrender. Compromise is more often a sign of true and profound creativity. But it takes painstaking activity and even heartfelt disagreement to come to healthy compromise. More often than not, this requires not merely a change in attitude, desires, and feelings but an even deeper *metanoia* that requires a high degree of humility.

Secondly, a deterrent to growth is the fear that some religious have of expressing love and joy and happiness in their religious life. The fear is sometimes centered around the idea of "cross-carrying," as if only a religious is called to live the life of the royal road of the cross. The fallacy of this idea has already been pointed out in an earlier chapter. No religious should have to be sad or to apologize for his choice of this state of life. Religious commitment means that a Christian has made the religious life the central core, the central mode of his very existence. A religious is not, for example, a teacher who lives the religious life. One chooses this state of life as a deep and thorough commitment that permeates everything he is, he does, he hopes for. A valid comparison can be made with the married state. A married person takes on that state in all its fullness — he (or she) lives the family life; works for the family; even wears a ring as a constant sign to others of commitment. But this is only one of many signs. Nor does a married person look longingly and ardently at another to whom he is not committed. The commitment has made a difference. But not a difference which deters the full and healthy growth of one's own personality or one's own love-of-God-and-neighbor-life. Just as a married person is a full-time married partner, so also religious life is a full-time commitment. There need be no fears, no apologies, no "humility-with-a-hook" attitudes that characterize such a religious commitment.

Finally, the third deterrent in religious life today that causes some problem is the attitude, especially among older religious, that because of the grace of religious commitment, individual religious do all things better than other Christians. The attitude can be aptly summarized in the words of a popular song: "I can do everything you can do — better." This, I think, is an illusion. Or at least it is a misconception of just what the meaning of religious life really is. Somehow religious over-identify with their communities and develop some grandiose ideas of what their roles in the Church are. Once again, religious have to realize that their religious commitment does not of itself make them professional persons. They become religious by profession, but not thereby professionals. There is a difference. The point is not that others do an apostolic work better or poorer than religious do. The criterion for performance is professional competency and not religious commitment. The real point of religious life is that if religious are also professional, then and only then do they bring to their apostolate a living witness to an aspect of the mystery of the Church that they and only they can give.

The very best antidote to any illusions of religious grandeur is to open one's eyes to any religious community, and to look around and see for oneself "the foolish things of the world" God has chosen: The wise and the not too wise; the intelligent and the not too intelligent; the strong and the not too strong; the noble and the not too noble. St. Paul's description of the early Christians is valid today, even for religious. If there is anything that should make religious different it is the fact that they strive to bring more love and more Christ-like charity to all that they do. They try to be greater lovers.

Some Principles for Future Growth:

No one today has a clear vision of just what the future will bring to the world or to the Church. If any religious has had mystical experience of insight into the future of religious life, he (or she) has not published such revelations. In the light of the past and in the existential experience of the present, at least some guiding principles can be suggested. It should be obvious to all by now that the Holy Spirit guides religious with his charismatic gifts. But at the same time to become more open to his inspirations, some principles are worthy of suggestion.

The first suggested principle may sound negative, but it is a norm that human experience over and over again has verified. The principle can be expressed in a truism: The publication of an enlarged edition of "rules and regulations" usually precedes the death-rattle of a dying organization. Customs, written rules, unwritten rules, procedures, practical norms, routines — all keep getting lumped together as time goes on, and new rules are constantly added to the old until absolutely no room is left for creativity. With the enlargement of rule books, creativity degenerates into conformity; energy is expended on learning and applying rules; success is measured in terms of conduct.

No sincere religious wants to be considered an iconoclast — to smash the images of the past out of recognition. Nor does any sincere religious believe that enacting more rules and regulations necessarily makes for better and holier religious. The first principle that should guide any sincere religious group looking to the future is that they refuse to be shackled by mere routine rules and regulations — no rules merely for the sake of rules, no matter how holy that rule may seem. Expressed more universally, this principle can be stated thus for religious: As much freedom as possible; as much regulation as is absolutely necessary.

Secondly, there has to be a very substantial continuity with the past. For all religious, this has to be a very conscious thing. Unless religious consider themselves founders of new religious types or groups or communities, there has to be a very conscious coordination with the past traditions that are essential or substantial to a religious group. Perhaps this oversight has caused some real problems in religious communities, almost to the point that self-identity is lost in some of their promotional literature. Or then again, some religious living in monastic communities suffer a role-diffusion and yearn to live the life of secular religious. Continuity with the past: with the life of the founder, the approval of the Church, the tradition of the group — all these are necessary if the rich development of the past and present are going to be permitted to grow in the future.

Thirdly, and finally, for every religious group experiment should be an important part of their religious life. I say an important part, not quantitatively but qualitatively important. Not that all religious are all the time experimenting. Nor that one cannot be a good, solid, holy religious unless engrossed in experiment. But rather, all religious should have a rational, sound, healthy attitude toward experiment in their own community and look upon experiment, under the inspiration of the Holy Spirit, as the risk to be taken for growth in faith — and hopefully in love.

Some Hopeful Future Developments:

The developments suggested here may seem, at first glance, not too conspicuous and quite a bit less than flamboyant. They are intended to be merely hopeful avenues of development that may well be converted, in time, into super-highways. Predictions at this time in the history of the Church may not be too meaningful. But these developments are not intended to be predictions. More accurately they are judgments based on changes already taking place in religious life.

One of the most salutary features of future development will be the fact that in many respects the religious life identity crisis will soon be over. The three basic forms of religious life will be expressed in more basically theological terms. As a result the functional roles of the three forms will be much clearer in the minds of religious themselves. Promotional literature will emphasize these functional roles and not confuse candidates as to the basic and fundamental meaning of different religious communities. For the time being, there may well continue to be an exodus from religious communities. Part of this has been caused by a role-diffusion within communities themselves. Similarly, once it is realized that monastic religious life is not the same as apostolic religious life, nor is apostolic the same as secular religious life — even though some particular types may situate between one and the other — there will be much more stability established. Of consoling import to all is the realization that there is as much need of monastic religious in the Church as there is of apostolic religious, and as much need of apostolic as there is of secular religious. In the recent past there was too much a tendency to think of all religious life as the same and that development meant change from monastic to secular form. Now we can see that this is a very narrow and non-theological view of religious life and that history does not prove this as fact. Optimistically, one can hope that all three forms — so necessary in the Church today and tomorrow — will continue to thrive strongly.

Once religious realize more fully that within the very heart of religious life there is a pulsing heartbeat pumping blood into a bloodstream ever causing change and improvement and good health to the entire body, and that change is to the benefit of the religious body, then we will see more active experimentation in religious life. Whether this will mean the evolution of new forms or deeper insight into the potential of the present forms, only time will tell. History has shown that both have taken place in the past.

Some of the older religious communities, because of the richness of their spiritual thrust, will be able to develop along with their original forms other forms as well. Some of this has historically already taken place, but because the development has not been clearly delineated, it has caused some pain and hard feeling in communities. However, time will ease these tensions especially because of the greater insight into the meaning of religious forms. For instance, there may well develop in time the three forms of religious life in Benedictine spirituality so that there will be Benedictine monastic religious, Benedictine apostolic religious, and Benedictine secular religious. Or perhaps, in time there may develop Jesuit apostolic religious along with Jesuit secular religious. Judging from past experience, however, it would seem that this would happen only under the inspiration of a person who has the same holiness, insight, imagination and originality of any religious founder. Nor does it seem likely that the trend will be the other way around: from secular institute to monastic religious. Perhaps the reason of historical evolution is the best argument against it as the historical evolution has been from monastic to apostolic and from apostolic to secular religious. Another reason is that in every religious community some members will be called and respond to the apostolate of prayer. In some apostolic religious communities, for instance, some members will be allowed, because of special circumstance, to make their entire apostolate one of praying for the apostolic works of its members. Under these circumstances there will hardly be need for transfer to another form of religious life.

Some specific items might, finally, be suggested as future developments. More and more monastic religious will take the lead in liturgical experimentation and reform. The Benedictine tradition in this regard has been magnificent. Monastic houses will be looked upon as the solid, firm, and stable rocks to which the "weary travelers" come out of the storms and squalls of life to find stability, serenity, peace which the world cannot give. They will be temporary retreats for other religious and laymen alike, much as they are in many Cistercian houses today.

Many apostolic religious will begin to unite their works and their houses, once they realize that all too frequently their only real difference is their religious name and the name of their founder. There will be much more sharing of property, personnel, equipment, and even specific houses once similarities, rather than dissimilarities, are stressed. Apostolic religious will be forced, because of the rise of professionalism in the secular world, to limit and specify their apostolates and cease looking upon themselves as universal apostles. They will become more specific and more catholic — that is, called as missionaries to all men, anywhere, but less and less universal.

And finally in the area in which prediction is most difficult, secular religious will flourish both in numbers and in variety for some time to come. As more and more Christians see the value of this form of religious life, they will be attracted to it. Many monastic and apostolic religious will also leave their communities and become secular religious. Many secular priests will take up the suggestion of Pope Paul and, seeing the value of living together as a community, make the commitment to secular religious life.

Concluding Remarks:

Maybe it isn't merely the popular movie hero who has to realize: "What's it all about, Alfie?" A young religious was overheard saying, "I was so absorbed in living that I never realized what life was all about." In a more reflective mood than ever before, religious are asking themselves: What's it all about? The reflective mood is good; the quiet and recollection it demands is good; the serenity with which it is associated is good. It's like the peace and quiet and coolness that comes after a rainstorm. The storm was there: unrest, disturbing winds, pelting rains, violent tossing and twisting, fears, tensions, even crushing hailstones. Some branches, large and small, and twigs too, have been broken from the ancient olive tree. In some places the ground is littered with wood, both dead and living. Now, most of the storm is over. The ancient olive tree is bursting with new life, all part of the whole mystery of life.

Religious are committed to mystery. Their very essence is to be mystery, a living mystery, as Cardinal Suhard said so well many years ago. Men should look at religious and wonder: How can they live this way in love together unless there is a God? Like every mystery which is revealed by God, there just is no full answer to that question without faith. If religious should stir people up at all, it should be by being what they are and what they should be: A community on God's special mission of love. That does make sense!

The spirit of every religious — yesterday's, today's, and tomorrow's — was excellently well summed up in the last written words of a "radical" religious whose eyes were set toward a distant horizon and riveted on a living, loving Omega Point:

"May the Risen Christ keep me young for God's greater glory — young, that is, optimistic, active, smiling, perceptive."

Pere P. Teilhard de Chardin, S.J.

INDEX